BUILDING PURPOSE-DRIVEN PROFITS

Damilola Tomiwa Fasinu

© 2024 Damiloa Tomiwa Fasinu

All rights reserved.

No part of this book, *Building Purpose-Driven Profits*, may be reproduced, distributed, or transmitted in any form or by any means, including photocopying, recording, or other electronic or mechanical methods, without the prior written permission of the author, except in the case of brief quotations embodied in critical reviews and certain other noncommercial uses permitted by copyright law.

Table Of Contents

DEDICATION   v

CHAPTER ONE   1
The Foundation of Purpose

CHAPTER TWO   9
Aligning Values and Vision

CHAPTER THREE   18
Identifying Your Niche

CHAPTER FOUR   25
Creating A Purpose-Driven Business Model

CHAPTER FIVE   35
Building A Purposeful Brand

CHAPTER SIX   42
Engaging Stakeholders and Building Community

CHAPTER SEVEN   52
Implementing Impact Metrics

CHAPTER EIGHT   61
Innovation For the Right Reasons

CHAPTER NINE   68
Ethical Leadership and Decision Making

CHAPTER TEN 83
Marketing With Purpose

CHAPTER ELEVEN 93
Scaling Sustainably

CHAPTER TWELEVE 103
The Future of Purpose-Driven Business

DEDICATION

To those who dare to dream and strive to create meaningful impact in the world. This book is dedicated to the passionate entrepreneurs who pursue purpose-driven profits, inspiring change while building thriving businesses. May your journey be filled with resilience, innovation, and the unwavering belief that success is best measured by the positive difference you make.

CHAPTER ONE

The Foundation of Purpose

The world of business has its unique twists and turns. There is no fixed blueprint to follow, and every entrepreneur's journey is different. However, in this field, one principle remains steadfast: the importance of purpose. For entrepreneurs like me, with extensive backgrounds in technology, real estate, agriculture and logistics, understanding and articulating a clear purpose can be the cornerstone of success. This chapter explores the significance of purpose in business, its profound impact on profitability, and how it can shape not only the trajectory of a company but also the lives of its employees, customers, and communities.

Defining Purpose in Business

At its core, purpose refers to the reason a business exists beyond making a profit. It is the underlying motivation that drives an organization to create value for its stakeholders. While profit is essential, purpose provides the guiding light that directs a company's efforts and decisions. In a world where consumers are increasingly conscious of the companies they support; a strong purpose can differentiate a brand in a crowded marketplace.

It's crucial to clarify that purpose does not replace profit; instead, it complements it. Businesses need to generate revenue to sustain operations, pay employees, and reinvest in growth. However, purpose-driven companies often find that their commitment to a higher mission can lead to increased profitability. This is not merely a theoretical concept; numerous studies support the assertion that purpose-driven organizations outperform their competitors financially.

The traditional view of business where profit was the sole focus is rapidly becoming obsolete. In today's market, consumers are more informed and discerning. They seek out brands that resonate with their values and contribute positively to society. This shift has led to a rise in purpose-driven businesses across various sectors, from tech startups to established corporations. For instance, companies like Patagonia and Ben & Jerry's have built strong identities around their commitment to social and environmental issues. Their purpose-driven approach not only enhances their brand image but also fosters customer loyalty, leading to sustained profitability.

The benefits of a purpose-driven approach are numerous and tremendous. It is both beneficial to the entrepreneur, founder, business and the society at large. They include:

Enhanced Employee Engagement: When employees understand and connect with the purpose of their organization, they are more likely to be engaged in their work. A clear purpose provides employees with a sense of belonging and meaning. According to a Gallup report, companies with engaged employees experience 21% greater profitability. Employees who feel connected to their company's purpose are more likely to go above and beyond, leading to increased productivity and innovation.

Stronger Customer Loyalty: Consumers today prioritize their purchasing decisions based on alignment with their personal values. Businesses that articulate their purpose effectively can forge deeper connections with their customers. A study by Nielsen found that 66% of global consumers are willing to pay more for sustainable brands. When customers perceive a brand as being purpose-driven, they are more likely to remain loyal, even in the face of competition.

Attracting Top Talent: In a competitive job market, attracting top talent is crucial. Job seekers increasingly prioritize organizations that have a clear purpose and demonstrate a commitment to making a positive impact. By showcasing a purpose-driven mission, businesses can attract and retain the best talent, creating a workforce that is not only skilled but also passionate about their work.

Increased Innovation: A purpose-driven culture fosters creativity and innovation. When employees are aligned with a mission, they are more likely to think outside the box and propose solutions that drive the business forward. This environment encourages risk-taking and experimentation, which can lead to the development of new products, services, and processes that ultimately enhance profitability.

Resilience in Challenging Times: Purpose can serve as a compass during challenging times. Companies with a strong sense of purpose are often more resilient in the face of adversity. When confronted with crises whether economic downturns, reputational challenges, or global pandemics purpose-driven organizations can rally their employees and stakeholders around a common mission, enabling them to navigate difficulties with greater cohesion and focus.

To illustrate the relationship between purpose and profitability, let's examine a few case studies of companies that have successfully integrated purpose into their business models.

Case Study 1: TOMS Shoes

TOMS Shoes is a prime example of a company that has built its brand around a compelling purpose: "One for One." For every pair of shoes sold, TOMS donates a pair to a child in need. This simple yet powerful mission has resonated with consumers, allowing TOMS to carve out a significant market share in the footwear industry. By aligning its business model with a social cause, TOMS not only generates revenue but also fosters brand loyalty and advocacy.

Case Study 2: Warby Parker

Warby Parker, an eyewear company, has a similar purpose-driven model. For every pair of glasses sold, they distribute a pair to someone in need. Their commitment to social responsibility has played a critical role in their rapid growth and success. In addition to their mission, Warby Parker has disrupted the eyewear industry by offering stylish, affordable glasses while providing a seamless online shopping experience. Their clear purpose has attracted a devoted customer base that values both quality and impact.

Case Study 3: Microsoft

Even established corporations like Microsoft have embraced the purpose of driving their business forward. Under CEO Satya Nadella, the company has shifted towards a mission of empowering every person and organization on the planet to achieve more. This renewed focus on purpose has led to a cultural transformation within the organization, enhancing employee engagement and driving innovation. As a result, Microsoft has experienced significant growth and profitability, demonstrating that even legacy companies can thrive by embracing purpose.

Case Study 4: Safaricom

Safaricom, Kenya's leading telecommunications provider has revolutionized the way people engage with technology through its mobile money platform, M-Pesa. Launched in 2007, M-Pesa was designed to provide financial services to individuals who previously lacked access to traditional banking. This purpose-driven initiative not only empowers millions of Kenyans to manage their finances but also stimulates economic growth in the region.

The company's commitment to enhancing the quality of life for its customers is at the heart of its mission. By prioritizing financial inclusion and leveraging technology, the business has cultivated a loyal customer base and experienced substantial growth in profitability. The company demonstrates that when a business aligns its purpose with the needs of the community, it can achieve remarkable success while driving social impact.

Case Study 5: The Body Shop Africa

The Body Shop, known for its ethical beauty products, has established a strong presence in Africa, emphasizing sustainability and social responsibility. The brand's mission is to enrich the lives of people and the planet, promoting fair trade and environmentally friendly practices. In South Africa, The Body Shop actively supports local communities by sourcing ingredients from small-scale farmers and advocating for fair trade practices.

This purpose-driven approach resonates deeply with consumers who prioritize ethical consumption. The Body Shop's commitment to environmental sustainability and social justice has not only enhanced its brand loyalty but has also contributed to its financial success in the region.

By focusing on a clear purpose that aligns with consumer values, The Body Shop demonstrates how businesses can thrive while making a positive difference in society.

Developing Your Purpose

For entrepreneurs, the journey to defining and embedding purpose in a business can be transformative. Here are some practical steps to guide you in developing your organization's purpose.

Reflect on Your Values: Begin by examining your personal values and the principles that drive your entrepreneurial journey. Consider what motivates you to start and grow your business. Your purpose should align with these core values to ensure authenticity.

Identify Stakeholder Needs: Engage with your stakeholders, employees, customers, partners, and the community to understand their needs and expectations. What challenges do they face? How can your business contribute to solving these issues? This feedback will help shape a purpose that resonates with those you serve.

Craft a Clear Mission Statement: Once you have a grasp of your values and stakeholder needs, create a mission statement that encapsulates your purpose. This statement should be concise, inspiring, and easily communicated. It will serve as a guiding framework for your business decisions and strategies.

Embed Purpose into Culture: To ensure your purpose permeates your organization, embed it into your company culture. Communicate your mission consistently through internal communications, training programs, and team-building activities. Encourage employees to live the purpose in their day-to-day roles.

Measure Impact: Establish metrics to measure the impact of your purpose-driven initiatives. Regularly assess how well your business is aligning with its mission and the tangible benefits it is creating for stakeholders. This will help you refine your approach and reinforce your commitment to purpose.

As we embark on this journey of building purpose-driven profits, it's essential to recognize that purpose is not just a trend; it is a powerful business strategy that can lead to sustainable success. By embedding a clear purpose into the fabric of your organization, you can enhance employee engagement, foster customer loyalty, attract top talent, and drive innovation.

The connection between purpose and profitability is undeniable. As entrepreneurs, we have the opportunity to create not just successful businesses but also positive change in the world. In the chapters that follow, we will delve deeper into specific strategies and case studies to illustrate how purpose-driven approaches can be integrated into various facets of business operations, paving the way for lasting impact and profitability.

CHAPTER TWO

Aligning Values and Vision

In the quest for purpose-driven profits, one of the most critical steps is defining your core values and aligning them with your business vision. This chapter will guide you through understanding the importance of values, how to define them, and practical steps to ensure they are woven into the fabric of your organization. We'll explore how aligned values, and vision can propel your business toward sustainable success, create a loyal customer base, and foster an inspiring workplace culture.

Understanding the Importance of Core Values

The first step is defining what core values mean. Core values are the fundamental beliefs and guiding principles that dictate behavior and action within an organization. They serve as a framework for decision-making and influence every aspect of a business, from hiring practices to customer interactions.

Core values provide a compass for leaders and employees, helping them make decisions that align with the organization's mission. They also aid in creating a strong culture. When values are shared and upheld, they foster a sense of belonging and unity among employees, creating a positive workplace culture. Customers and partners are more likely to engage with businesses whose values resonate with their own, leading to deeper relationships and loyalty. Finally, strong core values help differentiate your brand in a competitive market, making it more memorable and relatable. Consider companies like Patagonia, which emphasizes environmental responsibility, or Ben & Jerry's, known for its commitment to social justice. Their core values not only inform their business practices but also resonate deeply with their customer base, enhancing brand loyalty and driving profits.

Defining your core values is a critical step in building a purpose-driven business. To start, reflect on your personal values. Consider the principles that guide your life and the experiences that have shaped your beliefs; think about how these might translate into your business ethos. Engaging your team in this process is equally important. Conduct workshops or brainstorming sessions to gather diverse insights, fostering a sense of ownership and ensuring the values reflect a broader perspective.

As discussions unfold, identify key themes that emerge from the collective reflections. Look for patterns in the values that resonate most with you and your team, which may include themes like innovation, integrity, customer focus, and sustainability. Once you have a comprehensive list, prioritize these values to create a concise set, typically 3 to 5 core values that capture the essence of your business philosophy. Aim for values that are not only meaningful but also actionable and relatable to everyone in the organization.

Next, transform your prioritized values into clear statements. Each value statement should define the value itself while providing context about why it is vital to your organization. This clarity helps ensure that everyone understands the importance of these values and how they influence the overall direction of the business. By following this structured approach, you lay a strong foundation for aligning your values with your business vision, setting the stage for sustainable growth and purpose-driven success.

Aligning Values with Your Business Vision

Before you can align your core values with your vision, you must articulate what that vision is. A business vision is a forward-looking statement that outlines what you want your organization to achieve in the long term.

Once you have defined your vision, assess how your core values support and enhance it. Ask yourself, do your values empower the vision? Are there any discrepancies between your stated values and your vision? How can you ensure that your values are evident in your vision?

The next step is to communicate your values and vision. Effective communication is essential for ensuring that your values and vision are understood and embraced by all stakeholders. Consider the following strategies which are internal communication and external communication. For internal communication, use mechanisms such as team meetings, newsletters, and on boarding processes to educate employees about their values and vision. In external communication you can incorporate your values and vision into marketing materials, website content, and social media. This transparency builds trust with customers and partners.

Aligning values with your vision goes beyond communication; it requires integration into daily operations. Here's how to embed your values into the fabric of your organization. Start with your hiring practices; use your core values as a guiding framework to identify candidates who share similar beliefs. This alignment not only fosters a cohesive team culture but also enhances employee engagement and satisfaction. Additionally, incorporate your values into performance evaluations. By recognizing and rewarding employees who exemplify the organization's principles, you reinforce the importance of these values in daily operations and encourage others to follow suit.

Furthermore, establish a decision-making framework that explicitly considers how choices align with both your core values and the broader vision. This approach ensures that all levels of the organization are consistently guided by the same principles, making it easier to navigate challenges and maintain focus on long-term objectives. By embedding your core values into hiring, performance evaluations, and decision-making processes, you create a holistic system that strengthens the connection between values and vision, ultimately driving your business toward purpose-driven success.

Now, it is imperative to measure alignment and impact of whatever core values you have implemented. This helps you to gauge your efforts and understand what works and what needs to be changed. To ensure that your values and vision are not just words on a wall, establish KPIs that measure alignment and impact. These might include employee engagement scores, customer satisfaction ratings, retention rates and brand loyalty metrics.

Another step is to schedule regular check-ins to assess how well your organization is adhering to its core values and whether those values continue to support the business vision. Adjust as necessary to remain relevant and impactful. Create channels for feedback from employees and customers about how well your organization is living its values. This can include surveys, suggestion boxes, or focus groups. Use this feedback to refine your values and ensure they resonate with stakeholders. Examples of organizations that can be used as case studies include Zappos and TOMS. Zappos is renowned for its customer service, which is deeply rooted in its core values, including "Deliver WOW Through Service." The company empowers employees to make decisions that enhance customer experience, resulting in high customer loyalty and strong financial performance. TOMS has integrated its core value of social responsibility into its business model. For every pair of shoes sold, TOMS donates a pair to a child in need. This commitment to giving back not only aligns with its vision of improving lives but also attracts customers who share similar values.

Despite best efforts, misalignments and challenges in achieving alignment can occur. Common issues include:

Leadership Behaviors That Contradict Stated Values: When leaders fail to embody the core values of an organization, it can create significant distrust and confusion among employees. Leadership sets the tone for the company culture, and if leaders make decisions or exhibit behaviors that contradict the stated values, it sends a message that those values are not genuinely prioritized. For example, if a company emphasizes transparency but leaders are secretive about important decisions, employees may feel disillusioned and disengaged. This misalignment not only undermines the credibility of the leadership but can also lead to a toxic work environment where employees are reluctant to buy into the company's vision.

Employee Disengagement or Skepticism About Values: When employees perceive a disconnect between the organization's stated values and actual practices, they may become disengaged or skeptical about the values themselves. This skepticism can stem from witnessing behaviors that don't align with the stated principles, leading to a belief that the values are merely superficial or "corporate speak." Disengaged employees are less likely to be motivated, productive, or committed to the organization's goals. They may feel that their efforts are inconsequential in a culture that doesn't genuinely embrace its stated values, which can result in high turnover rates and diminished morale.

Inconsistencies in Customer Interactions:

Inconsistencies in customer interactions can also arise when there's discrepancy between an organization's values and its operational practices. If a company claims to prioritize customer satisfaction but fails to deliver on this promise in its service or support, customers will quickly notice. This dissonance can lead to a loss of trust and loyalty among customers, who expect brands to live up to their stated values. For instance, if a company promotes itself as environmentally conscious but engages in practices that harm the environment, it risks alienating its customer base. Over time, these inconsistencies can damage the brand's reputation and erode its competitive advantage, making it essential for organizations to ensure that their values are reflected in every interaction with customers.

There are several practical strategies for addressing misalignment in your structure. Some of them include:

Lead by Example: Leaders must embody the core values to inspire others.

Revisit Values Regularly: Periodically reassess and refresh your core values to ensure they remain relevant.

Promote Open Dialogue: Encourage conversations about values and vision among employees to address concerns and reinforce commitment.

The alignment of core values and business vision plays a crucial role in shaping an organization's long-term success. When values and vision are in harmony, they create a strong foundation for a purpose-driven culture that motivates employees and fosters customer loyalty. This alignment not only enhances brand identity but also positions the organization to adapt and thrive in an ever-evolving marketplace. These are some of the benefits that can be attained by this concept.

Building a Purpose-Driven Culture: When values and vision align, they create a purpose-driven culture that motivates employees and attracts customers. This culture fosters innovation, collaboration, and resilience, essential for navigating challenges and seizing opportunities.

Enhancing Brand Loyalty and Trust: Customers increasingly seek brands that reflect their values. By authentically embodying your core values, you build trust and loyalty, driving sustainable profits and long-term success.

Future-Proofing Your Business: As market dynamics shift, having a strong foundation of aligned values and vision enables your business to adapt and thrive. Purpose-driven organizations are more agile, allowing them to pivot in response to changing consumer preferences and societal expectations.

Aligning your core values with your business vision is not a one-time exercise but an ongoing journey. By clearly defining your values, ensuring they resonate with your vision, and embedding them into your organizational culture, you create a powerful foundation for purpose-driven profits. As you continue to grow and evolve, regularly revisit your values and vision, ensuring they remain aligned with the aspirations of your business and the needs of your stakeholders. Through this alignment, you will not only achieve financial success but also contribute positively to your community and the world at large.

CHAPTER THREE

Identifying Your Niche

There is a lot of discussion as to whether a business should stick to a broad range since its sole aim is to deliver results or identify its niche and grow there. To produce targeted results, identifying your niche is a vital step in building a purpose-driven business. A niche not only defines the specific market segment you intend to serve but also highlights the unique value your organization brings to that space. This chapter will guide you through the process of finding and validating a market need that resonates with your purpose, ensuring that your business is aligned with both your core values and the needs of your target audience. We'll explore techniques for market research, ways to evaluate potential niches, and methods for validating your business ideas through real-world testing.

Understanding the Concept of a Niche

A niche refers to a specific segment of the market that is characterized by distinct needs, preferences, or identities. Identifying a niche allows businesses to focus their efforts on serving a targeted audience rather than trying to appeal to everyone. This focus not only enhances marketing effectiveness but also improves customer satisfaction by addressing particular pain points.

The next question is, why is finding your niche important? Finding your niche is crucial for several reasons. First, a well-defined niche helps you stand out in a crowded marketplace. By catering to specific needs, you can differentiate your brand from competitors. Secondly, when you address particular problems or desires, you cultivate a loyal customer base that appreciates your specialized offerings. Finally, focusing on a niche allows for more efficient use of resources, enabling you to concentrate on the most promising opportunities.

Before diving into market research, it's essential to reflect on your business purpose and values. Your niche should resonate with what you stand for and the change you wish to bring to the world. Consider the following questions such as what issues or challenges are you passionate about solving? How do your values inform the kind of impact you want to make? What unique insights or experiences do you have that can inform your niche selection? These reflections will provide a foundation for identifying market needs that are not only viable but also aligned with your deeper mission.

Developing a purpose statement can clarify your intentions and guide your niche exploration. A well-crafted purpose statement succinctly articulates the "why" behind your business. It serves as a touchstone for evaluating potential niches and ensuring alignment with your broader goals.

When you have successfully answered the previous questions and have set the framework in place, you can go ahead to conduct your market research. Here are the steps to conducting market research:

Identifying Potential Niches: Begin your journey by brainstorming potential niches based on your reflections and purpose statement. Look for specific segments within larger markets that align with your passions and values. Use tools such as mind mapping or SWOT analysis (Strengths, Weaknesses, Opportunities, and Threats) to visualize different niche possibilities.

Secondary Research: Once you have a list of potential niches, engage in secondary research to gather existing information. Explore industry reports, academic journals, and market analysis publications to gain insights into market trends, consumer behaviors, and emerging needs. Pay attention to gaps in the market where existing solutions may fall short, as these can be fertile ground for niche opportunities.

Primary Research: While secondary research offers valuable insights, primary research provides a deeper understanding of your target audience. This can include surveys, interviews, and focus groups. To effectively conduct primary research, start by designing and distributing surveys to collect quantitative data about consumer preferences, pain points, and purchasing behaviors. Surveys allow you to gather measurable insights that can inform your understanding of the market. Additionally, conduct one-on-one interviews with potential customers or industry experts to gather qualitative insights. These conversations often reveal nuanced perspectives that surveys may overlook, providing deeper context to your findings. Furthermore, organizing small group discussions, or focus groups, can be incredibly beneficial. This interactive setting encourages participants to share their attitudes and reactions to specific ideas or concepts, generating valuable feedback that can help refine their offerings and better align them with market needs. By employing a combination of these methods, you can gain a comprehensive understanding of your target audience and their needs.

Evaluating and Prioritizing Niches

After gathering data, evaluate the potential of each niche based on market size and growth potential. Consider factors such as target audience, market trends and competition. In target audience, understand who are your potential customers, and how large is the audience? For market trends, are there trends or patterns that suggest a growing interest in this niche? Finally, to evaluate your competition, analyze existing competitors within the niche. What are their strengths and weaknesses? Is there room for another player?

Ensure that each niche under consideration aligns with your purpose and core values. Ask yourself whether pursuing this niche will allow you to fulfill your mission and whether it resonates with your intended impact. This alignment is essential for long-term satisfaction and sustainability. Assess the feasibility of pursuing each niche. Consider the resources, expertise, and time required to enter the market. Evaluate your current capabilities and determine whether you will need additional skills or partnerships to successfully operate in the niche.

Another vital aspect is validating your niche to enable you to prioritize. Once you've selected a niche, the next step is to validate your idea through the development of a Minimum Viable Product (MVP). An MVP is a simplified version of your product or service that allows you to test your concept with real customers while minimizing risk and investment. Then you proceed to test it with early adopters. Identify a group of early users within your target audience who are willing to test your MVP. Their feedback is invaluable for refining your offering. Use this opportunity to gather insights into usability, features, and overall satisfaction.

Based on the feedback from early adopters, make necessary adjustments to your product or service. This iterative process allows you to fine-tune your offering and ensures it better meets the needs of your target audience.

As you move forward with your niche, it's crucial to develop a compelling brand story that encapsulates your mission and values. Your brand story should communicate why you exist, what you stand for, and how you intend to make a difference in your chosen niche. This narrative will resonate with your audience and create an emotional connection. Create a cohesive visual identity that reflects your brand's essence. This includes logo design, color schemes, and typography, all of which should align with your purpose and target audience. Additionally, develop messaging that consistently communicates your values and the unique benefits of your niche offerings.

With a clear niche and strong brand identity, focus on targeted marketing strategies that reach your ideal customers. This might include content marketing, social media outreach, or partnerships with influencers in your niche. Tailor your messaging to address the specific needs and desires of your audience. Fostering a community around your niche can significantly enhance customer loyalty and engagement. Utilize social media platforms, online forums, and community events to connect with your audience. Encourage dialogue and interaction to strengthen relationships and foster a sense of belonging.

The market setting is ever-changing, and it's essential to stay attuned to new trends and shifts within your niche. Regularly conduct market analysis to identify emerging needs and evolving customer preferences. This vigilance allows you to adapt your offerings and maintain relevance. Continue to solicit feedback from your customers even after launching your specialized offering. Utilize surveys, reviews, and direct communication to understand their experiences and identify areas for improvement. This ongoing feedback loop will enable you to refine your products and services continuously. Two examples of businesses that can aid us to understand this concept properly are Warby Parker and Dollar Shave Club.

Warby Parker identified a niche within the eyewear market that focused on affordable, stylish glasses with a socially responsible business model. By addressing the pain point of high eyewear costs and providing a convenient online shopping experience, the company quickly gained traction. Their strong brand story and commitment to social impact, including donating a pair of glasses for every pair sold, resonated deeply with consumers, leading to rapid growth and loyalty.

Dollar Shave Club entered the competitive razor market by identifying a niche focused on convenience and affordability. Their humorous marketing approach and subscription model appealed to customers frustrated with high prices and the hassle of traditional retail. The company successfully validated its offering through a viral marketing campaign and gained a loyal customer base, ultimately leading to acquisition by Unilever.

Identifying your niche is a fundamental step in building a purpose-driven business that resonates with your audience and aligns with your values. By reflecting on your purpose, conducting thorough market research, and validating your offerings, you can carve out a space in the market that not only fulfills a genuine need but also enables you to make a meaningful impact. As you move forward, remain adaptable and committed to continuous improvement, ensuring that your business not only survives but thrives in the changing trends of your chosen niche. This alignment will ultimately lead to sustainable success and a fulfilling entrepreneurial journey.

CHAPTER FOUR

Creating A Purpose-Driven Business Model

In achieving full potential in your entrepreneurial journey, developing a sustainable business model is crucial. A well-defined business model not only outlines how your organization will operate and generate revenue but also ensures that your mission and values are integrated into every aspect of your business. This chapter will guide you through strategies for creating a business model that reflects your purpose, addresses your market needs, and positions your organization for long-term success.

Understanding Business Models

A business model is a framework that describes how a company creates, delivers, and captures value. It encompasses the organization's offerings, target market, revenue streams, cost structure, and key activities. Understanding the components of a business model is essential for aligning your operations with your purpose and ensuring sustainable growth.

A purpose-driven business model not only helps differentiate your organization in a competitive landscape but also fosters customer loyalty and employee engagement. When your business model aligns with your mission, it creates a strong narrative that resonates with stakeholders, enhancing brand identity and establishing a sense of trust.

Key components of a purpose-driven business model are necessary to ensure you are following the right framework while setting up a structure that works for you. They include:

Value Proposition: Your value proposition is a clear statement that outlines the unique benefits your product or service provides to customers. It should reflect your mission and address the specific needs of your target audience. To create an effective value proposition, consider what problems your offering solve? How does it improve the lives of your customers? What makes your product or service different from competitors?

Target Market: Defining your target market is essential for ensuring that your offerings resonate with the right audience. Identify the specific demographics, psychographics, and behaviors of your ideal customers. Understanding their preferences and pain points will help tailor your value proposition and marketing strategies.

Revenue Streams: A sustainable business model should outline various revenue streams that align with your purpose. Consider multiple avenues for generating income, such as direct sales of products or services, subscription models, partnerships or collaborations and donations or crowd funding for social initiatives.

Cost Structure: Understanding your cost structure is vital for maintaining financial sustainability. Identify fixed and variable costs associated with your operations, including production, marketing, distribution, and overhead expenses. Ensure that your cost structure supports your mission and allows for reinvestment in purpose-driven initiatives.

Key Activities and Resources: Define the key activities and resources necessary to deliver your value proposition effectively. These may include production processes, marketing and sales strategies, customer service and support and partnerships with suppliers or community organizations.

To create a purpose-driven business model, it's essential to infuse your mission into every operational aspect. This can include ethical sourcing of materials, sustainable production methods, fair labor practices and community engagement initiatives. By prioritizing ethical sourcing, businesses ensure that their raw materials are obtained responsibly, minimizing environmental impact and supporting suppliers who adhere to fair practices. Sustainable production methods reduce waste and energy consumption, fostering a healthier planet while appealing to environmentally conscious consumers. Fair labor practices ensure that workers receive equitable pay and safe working conditions, fostering loyalty and motivation within the workforce. Community engagement initiatives create meaningful connections with local stakeholders, reinforcing the brand's commitment to social responsibility. Together, these elements not only enhance a company's reputation but also attract customers who value integrity and purpose, ultimately driving long-term success and positive societal impact.

Engaging your employees in the mission is crucial for creating a cohesive purpose-driven culture. Involve them in discussions about the business model and encourage feedback on how to better align operations with your purpose. When employees feel connected to the mission, they are more likely to contribute positively to the organization's success.

Incorporate customer feedback into your business model to ensure it remains relevant and impactful. Create channels for customers to voice their opinions and experiences and use this input to refine your offerings and operations. By actively involving customers in the process, you can strengthen loyalty and enhance your brand's reputation.

Sustainable practices are also a game changer in a business model. Integrating these practices into your business model not only benefits the environment but also appeals to a growing segment of environmentally conscious consumers. Consider implementing practices such reducing waste through efficient production processes, utilizing renewable energy sources and offering eco-friendly products or services. Align your business model with social responsibility by supporting community initiatives or charitable causes that reflect your mission. This can include donating a percentage of profits to relevant organizations, volunteering time and resources to community projects and collaborating with local businesses to address social issues.

A purpose-driven business model must also be economically viable. Regularly assess your financial performance and adjust your strategies as needed to ensure long-term sustainability. Monitor your revenue streams, cost structure, and profitability to maintain a healthy balance between purpose and profit.

Validating Your Business Model

In this subsection, we will explore the essential steps for validating your business model, ensuring it aligns with market needs and stakeholder expectations. By employing strategic testing and feedback mechanisms, entrepreneurs can refine their concepts for greater success and sustainability.

Prototyping and Testing: Once you have developed your business model, it's essential to prototype and test your offerings. Create a minimum viable product (MVP) that reflects your value proposition and allows you to gather feedback from potential customers. Use this testing phase to validate assumptions and identify areas for improvement.

Gathering Customer Feedback: Engage with your target audience to gather feedback on your business model and offerings. Use surveys, interviews, or focus groups to understand their perceptions and preferences. This input will help you refine your model to better meet customer needs.

Adjusting Based on Insights: Based on the feedback you receive, be prepared to make adjustments to your business model. This iterative process ensures that your model remains aligned with both market demands and your purpose. Continuously monitor performance metrics to track progress and identify opportunities for improvement.

Creating a supportive ecosystem around your business model can amplify your impact and enhance sustainability. Identify potential partners who share your values and mission, whether they are suppliers, non-profit organizations, or complementary businesses. Collaborations can lead to shared resources, expanded reach, and greater social impact. Engage your stakeholders, including customers, employees, and community members, in discussions about your business model. Their insights can provide valuable perspectives and help you refine your strategies. Foster transparency and open communication to build trust and loyalty among your stakeholders.

For instance, IKEA has successfully integrated sustainability into its business model by prioritizing eco-friendly materials and processes. The company's commitment to reducing its environmental footprint is reflected in its product design, sourcing strategies, and waste reduction initiatives. By aligning its business model with a purpose-driven mission, IKEA has built a loyal customer base that values its commitment to sustainability. A second example is NIKANIKAN, which is a social enterprise based in Kenya that focuses on sustainable fashion. They produce high-quality clothing and accessories made from locally sourced materials, providing fair wages to artisans and supporting local communities. The company not only addresses the need for ethically produced fashion but also empowers women through skill development and economic independence. Their commitment to sustainability and community impact has resonated with socially conscious consumers, helping to build a loyal customer base.

Wecyclers, based in Nigeria, addresses the critical issue of waste management while promoting recycling in urban areas. The company employs a unique model that incentivizes low-income households to recycle by offering rewards for their waste. The company collects and processes recyclable materials, creating jobs and reducing the environmental impact of waste in communities. Their approach not only fosters environmental awareness but also empowers communities economically, demonstrating how a purpose-driven business can tackle social and environmental challenges simultaneously. Solar Sister operates in several African countries, including Uganda and Nigeria, and focuses on providing clean energy solutions to underserved communities. They empower women entrepreneurs to distribute solar energy products, such as solar lamps and cook stoves, in their communities. By combining social entrepreneurship with a focus on renewable energy, Solar Sister not only addresses energy poverty but also promotes gender equality and economic empowerment. Their mission-driven approach has garnered support from both consumers and investors, allowing them to expand their reach and impact. These examples highlight how purpose-driven businesses in Africa are making significant contributions to their communities while aligning with their missions and values.

Monitoring and adapting your business model is crucial for staying responsive to market changes and evolving customer needs. By continuously assessing performance and incorporating feedback, businesses can remain competitive and resilient in a dynamic landscape. There are several methods to achieve this:

Key Performance Indicators (KPIs): Establish key performance indicators (KPIs) to measure the success of your purpose-driven business model. These metrics can include financial performance, customer satisfaction, employee engagement, and social impact. Regularly assess your performance against these KPIs to ensure alignment with your mission and objectives.

Continuous Improvement: A purpose-driven business model requires ongoing evaluation and improvement. Stay attuned to market trends, customer feedback, and industry changes to adapt your model as needed. Embrace a mindset of continuous learning and be willing to pivot when necessary to maintain relevance and impact.

Leveraging Technology for Real-Time Insights: In today's digital age, utilizing technology can significantly enhance your ability to monitor and adapt your business model. Implement data analytics tools to gather real-time insights on customer behavior, market trends, and operational performance. By analyzing this data, you can make informed decisions quickly, identifying opportunities for improvement or innovation. Additionally, customer relationship management (CRM) systems can help you track customer interactions and feedback, ensuring that your offerings remain aligned with their evolving needs.

Building a Culture of Feedback and Experimentation: Fostering a culture of feedback and experimentation within your organization is crucial for continuous improvement. Encourage employees at all levels to share insights and propose new ideas based on their interactions with customers and their understanding of the market. Create safe spaces for experimentation, allowing teams to test new concepts without fear of failure. This agile approach enables your business to adapt rapidly and effectively to changes in the market, ensuring that your purpose-driven model remains relevant and impactful over time.

Creating a purpose-driven business model is essential for aligning your organization's operations with its mission and values. By understanding the key components of a business model and infusing your purpose into every aspect of your operations, you can build a sustainable framework that not only generates profits but also makes a meaningful impact. As you move forward, remain adaptable and committed to continuous improvement, ensuring that your business model evolves to meet the needs of your customers and the broader community. This alignment will ultimately lead to lasting success and a fulfilling journey in your entrepreneurial endeavors.

CHAPTER FIVE

Building A Purposeful Brand

Revenue is important but leaving an impact behind has been proven to stand the tests of time. In an increasingly competitive marketplace, where consumers are more informed and discerning than ever, building a purposeful brand is essential for long-term success. A purposeful brand goes beyond mere profit generation; it resonates with the values and aspirations of its audience, fostering a deeper connection that inspires loyalty and advocacy. This chapter delves into crafting a compelling brand narrative that communicates your purpose and connects authentically with your audience, offering actionable insights and strategies drawn from my own entrepreneurial journey.

Understanding the Essence of Purpose

Before crafting your brand narrative, it's crucial to define what your purpose is. This involves asking foundational questions: Why does your business exist? What change do you want to create in the world? A clear and authentic brand purpose serves as the North Star for your organization, guiding decision-making and strategic direction. For instance, brands like Patagonia and TOMS have established their purposes around environmental sustainability and social impact, respectively. By articulating a clear purpose, you not only differentiate your brand from competitors but also create a strong emotional bond with your audience.

Authenticity is key when it comes to purpose-driven branding. Consumers today are adept at spotting insincerity, and a lack of genuine commitment to your stated purpose can damage your brand's reputation. Building an authentic brand narrative requires introspection and a commitment to aligning your practices with your purpose. Consider the example of Ben & Jerry's, which has built its brand around social justice issues. Their commitment to their cause is reflected not only in their marketing but also in their operational practices, making their narrative credible and compelling.

Numerous individuals struggle with crafting a brand narrative. Some think it's complex, unnecessary or they don't know where to start. There are several techniques you can test out in determining what works well for you in creating your brand story.

One is using storytelling as a tool for connection. At the heart of any effective brand narrative is storytelling. Stories are powerful tools that evoke emotions, making complex ideas relatable and memorable. To craft a compelling brand narrative, you should focus on three key elements: the protagonist (your brand), the challenge (the problem you aim to solve), and the resolution (how your brand contributes to the solution). For example, Nike's "Just Do It" campaign embodies this storytelling approach by showcasing athletes who overcome personal challenges through determination and perseverance. This narrative not only inspires individuals but also positions Nike as a brand that champions resilience and achievement.

A second step is to pinpoint your audience and ensure they are the right one. Understanding your target audience is vital for crafting a narrative that resonates. Conduct thorough research to gain insights into their values, motivations, and pain points. Segment your audience to tailor your messaging effectively, ensuring that your narrative speaks directly to their needs and aspirations.

Finally, is to develop your unique voice. Your brand's voice is how you communicate your narrative and purpose. It should be consistent across all platforms whether in social media posts, website copy, or customer service interactions. Consider the tone and style that align with your brand identity. Are you friendly and approachable, or authoritative and professional? Your voice should reflect your brand's personality and values.

Communicating Your Purpose Across Channels

The rise in social media and apparent world globalization has occasioned the rise of several channels of communication. This change has even affected person communication and how we pass information to our audience every day. Consistence in passing information across several channels has never been so necessary as now.

Once you've crafted your brand narrative, it's essential to communicate it consistently across all channels. Inconsistent messaging can confuse your audience and dilute your brand's impact. Ensure that your purpose is woven into your marketing materials, social media posts, customer interactions, and even product design. Visual elements such as your logo, color palette, and typography play a crucial role in conveying your brand purpose. A well-designed visual identity should reflect your core values and create an emotional response. For instance, a brand focused on eco-friendliness might use earthy tones and organic shapes, while a tech-forward brand might opt for sleek, modern aesthetics.

Social media platforms provide an ideal space for dynamic storytelling. Use these channels to share your brand's journey, highlight customer stories, and showcase community involvement. Engaging content, such as behind-the-scenes videos, live Q&A sessions, and impactful imagery, can foster a sense of community and amplify your brand's purpose. Regularly interact with your audience through comments and messages to build a stronger connection.

Create targeted marketing campaigns that align with your brand purpose. These campaigns can focus on specific social or environmental issues relevant to your mission, encouraging your audience to participate actively. For example, consider running a campaign where a portion of sales goes to a cause you support, inviting customers to be part of the change. This not only reinforces your purpose but also builds customer loyalty and engagement. Leverage email marketing to communicate your purpose directly to your audience. Share stories, updates, and insights that reflect your brand's mission and values. Use newsletters to highlight initiatives, showcase customer impact, and provide exclusive content related to your purpose. Personalized emails can strengthen relationships, making your audience feel valued and connected to your brand's journey.

Content marketing is a powerful way to share your brand narrative. Through blog posts, videos, podcasts, and social media content, you can engage your audience by providing value while reinforcing your purpose. Share stories of impact, customer testimonials, and behind-the-scenes insights that illustrate how your brand is making a difference.

A purposeful brand thrives on community. By fostering a community around shared values, you can deepen connections with your audience. Consider creating platforms for customers to engage with each other, such as forums, social media groups, or events that reflect your brand's purpose. Encourage your audience to share their own stories related to your brand's purpose. User-generated content not only amplifies your message but also strengthens community ties. Highlighting customer stories reinforces the idea that your brand is part of a larger movement, creating a sense of belonging among your audience.

Partnering with other brands that share your values can enhance your brand narrative and expand your reach. Collaborative initiatives, whether through co-branded products, joint campaigns, or community events can amplify your purpose and introduce your brand to new audiences.

To assess the effectiveness of your purposeful branding efforts, establish clear KPIs. These may include metrics related to brand awareness, customer loyalty, social impact, and community engagement. Regularly reviewing these indicators will help you gauge whether your narrative resonates and aligns with your audience's expectations. Feedback is essential for refining your brand narrative. Actively seek input from customers, employees, and stakeholders to understand their perceptions of your brand's purpose. Use surveys, focus groups, and social listening tools to gather insights that can inform your narrative and overall strategy.

The business landscape is constantly evolving, and so are consumer expectations. Stay attuned to market trends and shifts in consumer behavior. Adapt your brand narrative as needed to remain relevant and responsive. For instance, if a new social issue emerges that aligns with your purpose; consider how your brand can engage with it authentically.

Building a purposeful brand is not just a trend; it's a necessity for businesses seeking sustainable growth and genuine customer loyalty. By crafting a compelling brand narrative that clearly communicates your purpose, engaging authentically with your audience, and continually refining your approach, you can create a brand that not only thrives in the marketplace but also makes a meaningful impact.

As you embark on this journey, remember that a purposeful brand is built on authenticity, connection, and commitment. The effort you invest in understanding and communicating your purpose will not only enhance your brand's reputation but also contribute to a larger narrative of positive change in the world. Embrace the opportunity to build a brand that resonates with your audience and stands as a testament to your values, inspiring others to join you in creating a better future.

CHAPTER SIX

Engaging Stakeholders and Building Community

Times are changing and the business sector is not left out. In the modern business settings, success is no longer solely defined by profit margins and market share. The most thriving enterprises recognize the importance of building and engaging a community of stakeholders which encompass customers, employees, partners, and even broader social networks who share a common vision. This chapter explores practical strategies for cultivating these relationships, illustrating how to create a robust community that aligns with your brand's purpose and values. To bring these concepts to life, we'll weave in a fictional story that exemplifies these principles in action.

What is the Importance of Community

The power of stakeholder engagement or engaging stakeholders is not just a nice-to-have; it's essential for sustainable growth. When stakeholders feel connected to your brand, they become advocates who amplify your message and contribute to your mission. This engagement fosters loyalty and trust, leading to increased customer retention and employee satisfaction. Moreover, a strong community can serve as a valuable source of feedback and innovation, driving your business forward.

To effectively engage stakeholders, it's vital to establish a shared vision that resonates with your community. This vision should reflect your brand's purpose and values, providing a clear understanding of what you stand for. By aligning your goals with the aspirations of your stakeholders, you create a sense of belonging and shared responsibility that strengthens your community.

The Story of "Green Wave"

Let's illustrate these principles through the fictional story of Green Wave, a sustainable clothing brand founded by Emma, a passionate entrepreneur dedicated to environmental conservation. Emma's vision was to create stylish, eco-friendly apparel while fostering a community that shared her commitment to sustainability. From the outset, Emma understood the importance of defining her brand's purpose. She spent time articulating what Green Wave stood for: creating clothing that minimized environmental impact, supporting ethical manufacturing, and advocating for social responsibility. This clarity served as the foundation for all future engagement with stakeholders.

For her next step, she built a framework for cultivating relationships with customers. She launched Green Wave with a clear strategy to create an inclusive community by engaging customers. She created an online platform where customers could not only shop but also share their stories about why sustainability mattered to them. The website featured a blog section where customers could contribute articles on eco-friendly practices, showcasing their commitment to the brand's mission. To deepen the connection with her customers, Emma organized local community events such as clothing swaps, workshops on sustainable fashion, and beach clean-ups. These events not only promoted the company's products but also encouraged customers to engage directly with each other and the brand. Attendees often shared their experiences on social media, amplifying their reach and reinforcing community ties.

Recognizing that her employees were crucial stakeholders, she prioritized creating a work environment that reflected the organization's values. She implemented a transparent hiring process, focusing on candidates who were passionate about sustainability and community engagement. This alignment fostered a culture of shared purpose within the company. Emma encouraged employees to develop initiatives that contributed to the brand's mission. One employee, Mia, proposed a program to recycle used clothing into new products. Emma supported this idea, allowing Mia to lead workshops where employees could brainstorm sustainable practices. This not only empowered the team but also created a sense of ownership and pride in their work.

She knew that building a community extended beyond her own business. She sought partnerships with other brands and organizations that shared Green Wave's vision. Collaborations could amplify their collective impact, whether through co-branded products or joint campaigns. One successful partnership was with local non-profit focused on ocean conservation. Green Wave designed a limited-edition line of apparel, with a portion of sales going to support the organization's initiatives. This collaboration resonated with customers and increased awareness for both entities, illustrating the power of shared missions.

Emma also recognized the importance of engaging in advocacy efforts. Her company became involved in local sustainability initiatives, supporting legislation that promoted eco-friendly practices. By aligning the brand with broader movements, she positioned Green Wave as a leader in the sustainable fashion space, attracting like-minded stakeholders.

Here are practical strategies for building community that we can imbibe and was instrumental to Green Wave's success.

Utilizing social media:

Social media is a powerful tool for engaging stakeholders and building community. Green Wave actively used platforms like Instagram and Facebook to showcase customer stories, share sustainability tips, and promote community events. Emma encouraged followers to tag the brand in their posts, creating a sense of connection and shared identity.

Creating a Feedback Loop: Listening to stakeholders is critical for fostering community. Green Wave established a feedback loop where customers could share their thoughts on products, sustainability practices, and brand initiatives. Emma used surveys and polls to gather insights, ensuring that the community felt heard and valued.

Establishing Loyalty Programs:

To reward loyal customers, Green Wave implemented a loyalty program that incentivized sustainable practices. For instance, customers could earn points by recycling old clothing or attending community events. This program not only encouraged repeat business but also reinforced the brand's commitment to sustainability.

Hosting Virtual Events: In response to the growing trend of remote engagement, Emma organized virtual events like webinars and online workshops focused on sustainable living. These events allowed Green Wave to reach a broader audience, fostering community engagement regardless of geographic barriers.

As Green Wave continued to grow, so did its community. The combination of engaged customers, empowered employees, and meaningful partnerships created a vibrant ecosystem that supported the brand's mission.

Emma made it a priority to celebrate milestones with the community. Whether it was reaching a sales target or launching a new product line, she would share these achievements with stakeholders, expressing gratitude for their support. This not only fostered a sense of belonging but also reinforced the idea that the community was integral to the company's success.

There were challenges but her adaptability and flexibility came in handy. When the COVID-19 pandemic hit, Emma quickly adapted to the changing landscape. She pivoted to online sales and virtual events, ensuring that the community remained connected. The company launched a campaign encouraging customers to share how they were practicing sustainability during lockdown, further solidifying the brand's relevance and commitment.

As the community flourished, Green Wave began to attract attention beyond its local market. The brand was featured in sustainability publications, leading to collaborations with influences and expansion into new markets. Emma's dedication to engaging stakeholders had created a ripple effect, amplifying Green Wave's mission and impact.

To gauge the effectiveness of her community-building efforts, she established metrics to track stakeholder engagement. These included social media interactions, event attendance, customer feedback, and sales data. Regularly reviewing these metrics helped Emma refined her strategies and continued fostering a strong community. The organization conducted annual surveys to assess stakeholder satisfaction, focusing on employees, customers, and partners. The feedback collected allowed the team to identify areas for improvement and ensure that the community remained aligned with the brand's mission.

As Green Wave grew, so did the needs and expectations of its community. Emma recognized the importance of staying attuned to these changes. Regularly engaging with stakeholders through focus groups and discussions helped her adapts to evolving preferences and ensures that the community continued to thrive.

The journey of Green Wave illustrates that building a purposeful brand is not a solitary endeavor; it requires cultivating relationships with a diverse community of stakeholders. By engaging customers, empowering employees, and forging meaningful partnerships, businesses can create a vibrant ecosystem that shares a common vision.

Cultivating a Culture of Inclusivity

Building a thriving community around your brand necessitates fostering a culture of inclusivity that welcomes diverse perspectives and backgrounds. This not only enriches the community but also enhances creativity and innovation. Here's how you can cultivate an inclusive culture within your organization and among your stakeholders.

Embracing Diversity in Hiring: A truly inclusive community begins with a diverse workforce. As Emma expanded Green Wave, she prioritized hiring individuals from various backgrounds, experiences, and identities. She implemented inclusive hiring practices, ensuring that job postings were accessible and appealing to a wide range of candidates. By creating a diverse team, Emma brought in unique perspectives that enriched the brand's mission and engagement strategies. To implement this, develop partnerships with organizations that focus on diversity in employment. Attend job fairs that emphasize inclusivity and reach out to communities underrepresented in your industry.

Creating Safe Spaces for Dialogue: To nurture inclusivity, it's essential to create safe spaces where all stakeholders feel comfortable expressing their ideas, concerns, and feedback. Emma established regular town hall meetings at Green Wave, where employees and community members could voice their thoughts and share experiences related to sustainability and social issues. These gatherings not only fostered open communication but also allowed for collaborative brainstorming on how the brand could better serve its community. This approach strengthened relationships and built a sense of belonging among stakeholders. To apply this, implement anonymous feedback mechanisms, such as suggestion boxes or digital surveys, to allow stakeholders to share their insights without fear of judgment.

Amplifying Underrepresented Voices:

Green Wave actively sought to amplify underrepresented voices within the community. Emma collaborated with local activists, artists, and influencers who aligned with the brand's mission. By showcasing their stories and contributions through social media features, blog posts, and events, she highlighted diverse perspectives and fostered a sense of solidarity. This approach not only enriched the company's narrative but also demonstrated a commitment to inclusivity, encouraging more stakeholders to engage with the brand. In your framework, launch initiatives that spotlight diverse voices, such as mentorship programs or scholarships for underrepresented individuals pursuing careers in sustainable fashion or any other relevant field of your choice.

Promoting Continuous Learning and Growth:

Fostering an inclusive culture requires ongoing education and growth. Emma implemented regular training sessions for employees on topics like cultural competency, unconscious bias, and inclusive communication. These sessions not only educated the team but also created a shared language around inclusivity, enhancing collaboration and understanding. By prioritizing continuous learning, she ensured that the culture at Green Wave remained adaptive and open to new ideas, creating an environment where everyone felt empowered to contribute. As a founder or entrepreneur, encourage employees and community members to share their own learning experiences and resources, fostering a culture of knowledge-sharing and growth.

Celebrating Diversity Through Events: To reinforce the importance of inclusivity, Emma organized events that celebrated diverse cultures and perspectives within the community. Green Wave hosted cultural festivals, workshops, and panel discussions featuring speakers from various backgrounds. These events not only educated attendees but also showcased the richness of diversity, enhancing community engagement. To achieve this, collaborate with local cultural organizations to co-host events that celebrate heritage, traditions, and social issues relevant to your community.

Engaging stakeholders fosters loyalty, drives innovation, and amplifies impact, positioning your brand as a leader in your industry. As you embark on your own journey to build community, remember that genuine relationships, shared values, and open communication are the cornerstones of success. By embracing these principles, you can create a thriving community that not only supports your business objectives but also contributes to a better, more sustainable world.

CHAPTER SEVEN

Implementing Impact Metrics

In the quest for sustainable business practices, measuring success has evolved beyond traditional financial metrics. Today, purpose-driven entrepreneurs recognize the necessity of integrating social and environmental impact into their performance evaluations. This chapter delves into the significance of impact metrics, outlines various methods for measuring both financial and social performance, and provides a framework for implementing these metrics effectively in your organization.

The Importance of Impact Metrics

As purpose-driven entrepreneurs, we understand that our ventures do more than generate profits; they also have the potential to enact positive change in society and the environment. However, to truly realize this potential, we must be able to measure and communicate our impact effectively.

There are important reasons why we must carry this out effectively and frequently if possible. First, it is effective in attracting stakeholders to the business. Investors, customers, and employees are increasingly looking for businesses that align with their values. By demonstrating a commitment to social impact through measurable metrics, you can attract and retain these stakeholders.

Impact metrics provide valuable data that can inform strategic decisions. Understanding the social and environmental consequences of your business practices allows you to optimize operations for greater positive outcomes. It is also used for enhancing accountability. Implementing impact metrics fosters a culture of transparency and accountability within your organization. By regularly assessing your performance against these metrics, you can ensure that your business stays true to its mission and values.

The process of measuring impact allows for reflection and learning. By evaluating what works and what doesn't, you can make informed adjustments to improve both financial and social outcomes.

Before diving into the measurement process, it's essential to define the metrics that align with your organization's mission and goals. Here are some critical steps to guide you:

Identify Key Objectives: Start by clarifying the primary objectives of your business. What social or environmental issues do you aim to address? Your impact metrics should directly reflect these objectives. For instance, if your mission is to reduce carbon emissions, you might measure the reduction in greenhouse gas output attributable to your operations.

Align with Stakeholders: Engage with stakeholders including employees, customers, community members, and investors to understand their perspectives on what constitutes success. This engagement can provide insight into the metrics that will resonate most with your audience.

Choose Relevant Metrics: Select metrics that are both meaningful and measurable. Consider using established frameworks, such as the UN Sustainable Development Goals (SDGs) or the Global Reporting Initiative (GRI), which provide standardized indicators for assessing social and environmental performance. Some key categories to consider include financial performance, social impact and environmental impact. In financial performance, components such as revenue growth, profit margins, and return on investment (ROI) come into play. Social impact involves community engagement, employee satisfaction, diversity and inclusion metrics while environmental impact can refer to resource consumption, waste reduction, and carbon footprint.

Establish Baselines and Targets: To measure progress, establish baselines for each metric and set realistic target. Baselines represent your current performance levels, while targets should be ambitious yet achievable, encouraging your team to strive for improvement.

Once you have defined your impact metrics, the next step is to implement measurement methods. Here are several approaches to consider in understanding what mechanisms suit you.

Collect qualitative and quantitative data from stakeholders through surveys and feedback forms. These tools can help assess customer satisfaction, employee engagement, and community perceptions of your impact. Secondly, utilize data analytics to track key performance indicators (KPIs) related to financial and social performance. Software solutions can help aggregate data from various sources, enabling you to visualize trends and identify areas for improvement.

Benchmarking is a powerful method for assessing your organization's impact by comparing your metrics to industry standards or best practices. This involves researching and identifying key performance indicators (KPIs) relevant to your sector and analyzing how your business measures up. By participating in industry surveys or collaborating with sector organizations, you can gather valuable data on the performance of similar enterprises. This comparative analysis not only helps identify gaps and opportunities for improvement within your own operations but also sets a baseline for expected performance. Establishing these benchmarks allows you to evaluate your progress over time and reinforces your commitment to continuous improvement, driving both accountability and transparency within your organization.

Another effective means is participatory impact assessment which involves engaging stakeholders such as employees, customers, and community members in the evaluation process. By inviting these groups to contribute their perspectives, you can gain deeper insights into the real-world effects of your business practices. This approach often includes workshops, focus groups, or community forums where stakeholders can share their experiences, feedback, and suggestions for improvement. Not only does this method enhance the validity of your impact measurements, but it also fosters a sense of ownership and collaboration among participants. By involving stakeholders in the assessment process, you ensure that the metrics reflect the true impact of your business and align with the values and needs of the communities you serve. This collaborative approach can strengthen relationships and build trust, ultimately enhancing your organization's credibility and commitment to social responsibility.

Documenting case studies can provide compelling evidence of your impact. Share stories that illustrate how your business has positively affected individuals or communities, highlighting both qualitative and quantitative outcomes. Consider engaging third-party organizations to evaluate your impact. These assessments can lend credibility to your metrics and provide an objective perspective on your performance.

Establish a system for continuous monitoring of your metrics. Regular reviews allow you to track progress, identify challenges, and adjust strategies as necessary to enhance your impact.

Communicating Your Impact

Once you've measured your impact, the next step is to communicate your findings effectively. Transparency is pivotal to building trust with stakeholders. Here are some strategies to consider:

Annual Impact Reports: Create an annual impact report that outlines your financial performance alongside your social and environmental contributions. Use clear visuals, such as graphs and charts, to present data in an engaging manner.

Digital Platforms: Leverage digital platforms, such as your website and social media, to share real-time updates on your impact metrics. This ongoing communication can foster a sense of community and encourage stakeholder engagement.

Stakeholder Engagement: Organize and host events or forums to discuss your impact with stakeholders. These gatherings provide an opportunity to share successes, gather feedback, and strengthen relationships within your community.

Case Study: A Purpose-Driven Business

To illustrate the implementation of impact metrics, let's examine a hypothetical purpose-driven business: EcoTech Solutions. This company specializes in developing sustainable technology solutions for businesses seeking to reduce their environmental footprint.

First in line were objectives and metrics. EcoTech Solutions identified three primary objectives namely to reduce energy consumption for clients by 30% over five years, increase employee engagement and satisfaction by fostering a culture of sustainability and contribute to local environmental initiatives by partnering with community organizations.

To measure these objectives, the company established the following metrics:

Energy Reduction: Percentage decrease in energy consumption for clients.

Employee Engagement: Employee satisfaction survey results and retention rates.

Community Impact: Number of partnerships with local organizations and funds contributed to environmental projects.

The organization utilized various methods to track and monitor these metrics:

Surveys were conducted bi-annually to gauge employee engagement and satisfaction.

Data analytics software was employed to monitor energy consumption metrics for clients, allowing for real-time adjustments and reporting.

Regular meetings were held with community partners to assess the impact of collaborative initiatives.

Each year, EcoTech published an annual impact report highlighting both financial success and social contributions. The report showcased the reduction in energy consumption across their client base, employee satisfaction scores, and details of community projects funded through partnerships. These reports were shared on their website and at stakeholder meetings.

While implementing impact metrics can yield significant benefits, challenges often arise. We will discuss common obstacles and strategies to overcome them. First are data collection difficulties. Collecting reliable data can be time-consuming and complex. To solve this, streamline data collection processes through automation and invest in tools that simplify tracking and reporting.

A second obstacle is balancing financial and social metrics. Striking the right balance between financial performance and social impact can be challenging. Ensure that your metrics are integrated rather than siloed or in scattered components. Consider developing composite scores that reflect both financial and social performance. Another common issue is stakeholder buy-in. Gaining buy-in from stakeholders can be difficult, especially if they prioritize financial metrics.

To resolve this, educate stakeholders on the long-term value of social impact. Highlight case studies and data that demonstrate how purpose-driven strategies can lead to enhanced financial performance over time.

Implementing impact metrics is essential for purpose-driven entrepreneurs seeking to align their financial performance with their social and environmental contributions. By defining relevant metrics, employing effective measurement methods, and communicating impact transparently, businesses can drive meaningful change while achieving sustainable profits.

As we move forward in discovering how we can build purpose-driven profits, let us embrace the challenge of measuring impact with the same vigor we apply to our financial goals. Together, we can build a future where purpose and profit go hand in hand, driving not only business success but also a positive transformation in our communities and the world at large.

CHAPTER EIGHT

Innovation For the Right Reasons

As an entrepreneur or individual seeking to excel in business, innovation is often celebrated as the holy grail of growth and competitive advantage. However, not all innovation is created equal. The true challenge lies in fostering a culture of innovation that is driven by purpose which is one that aligns with the core values of an organization and meets genuine societal needs. In this chapter, we will explore how to cultivate an environment where innovation flourishes, but not just for the sake of novelty. Instead, we will focus on innovation that serves a greater purpose and leads to sustainable profits.

The Purpose-Driven Paradigm

At the heart of purpose-driven innovation is the idea that businesses can thrive while also contributing positively to society. Purpose-driven organizations prioritize long-term impact over short-term gains. They seek to address societal challenges through their products and services, aligning their innovations with the values of their stakeholders which include customers, employees, investors, and the communities in which they operate.

Before we dive into strategies for fostering a culture of innovation, it's crucial to define what we mean by "purpose." A clear purpose acts as a compass for decision-making and innovation. It goes beyond profit margins and shareholder value to encompass broader societal and environmental goals. For example, a company like Patagonia has woven environmental sustainability into its core purpose, guiding its product development and marketing strategies. This alignment not only resonates with their customer base but also fosters loyalty and drives long-term success.

How do we create an environment for purposeful innovation in our business structures? First, innovation for the right reasons starts at the top. Leaders must embody the organization's purpose and demonstrate a commitment to innovation that reflects it. This involves not only verbal affirmation but also actions that support and prioritize purpose-driven initiatives. When leaders actively participate in the innovation process in ways such as investing resources, time, and energy, they inspire a culture where innovation is seen as a shared responsibility.

A culture of innovation thrives in an environment where ideas can flow freely. Open dialogue fosters creativity and collaboration, allowing employees at all levels to contribute their perspectives. Establishing regular brainstorming sessions, innovation workshops, and cross-departmental teams can break down silos and stimulate diverse ideas. This inclusivity is vital; the best innovations often come from unexpected sources.

Fear of failure can stifle innovation. To counter this, organizations must cultivate a mindset that views failure as a learning opportunity. By creating a safe space for experimentation, businesses encourage employees to take calculated risks. Celebrating both successes and failures can reinforce the idea that innovation is a journey, not a destination. This cultural shift encourages teams to iterate on their ideas, ultimately leading to more refined and impactful innovations. Purpose should be embedded into every stage of the innovation process which is from ideation to execution. This can be achieved through frameworks that prioritize purpose alongside feasibility and viability. For instance, organizations can adopt design thinking methodologies that focus on understanding user needs and aligning solutions with societal challenges. Tools like the Business Model Canvas can also help teams visualize how their innovations contribute to a broader purpose.

The new motto in this current dispensation is collaboration and not sole competition. Engaging with external stakeholders, customers, community members, and non-profit organizations can provide valuable insights into societal needs and trends. Collaborations can lead to innovative solutions that address these needs effectively. For instance, companies like Unilever have successfully partnered with NGOs to develop products that improve health and hygiene in underserved communities. Such collaborations not only drive innovation but also enhance brand reputation and customer loyalty.

Measuring Purpose-Driven Innovation

To ensure that innovation aligns with purpose, organizations must develop metrics that capture both qualitative and quantitative outcomes. Traditional performance indicators, such as revenue and market share, should be complemented with measures that reflect social and environmental impact. For example, measuring customer satisfaction alongside the positive effects of a product on community health can provide a more holistic view of success.

Key Performance Indicators (KPIs) should include components such as

Impact Metrics: Assess how innovations contribute to societal goals, such as improved access to education or reduced carbon emissions.

Employee Engagement: Track employee involvement in innovation initiatives and their alignment with the company's purpose. High engagement often correlates with more innovative outputs.

Customer Feedback: Solicit input from customers about how well new products and services meet their needs and align with their values.

Sustainability Indices: Evaluate the environmental impact of innovations through sustainability metrics, such as resource usage and waste reduction.

By integrating these metrics into the overall performance evaluation process, organizations can maintain a strong focus on purpose-driven innovation while ensuring accountability.

Case Studies of Purpose-Driven Innovation

To illustrate the principles discussed, let's examine a few organizations that exemplify purposeful innovation.

Tesla: Revolutionizing Transportation

Tesla is a prime example of a company that has harnessed innovation for a greater purpose. Founded with the mission to accelerate the world's transition to sustainable energy, Tesla's innovations in electric vehicles and battery technology are rooted in environmental stewardship. By aligning its product development with this mission, Tesla has not only disrupted the automotive industry but has also positioned itself as a leader in sustainability.

TOMS Shoes: A Model for Social Entrepreneurship

TOMS Shoes pioneered the "one for one" model, where for every pair of shoes sold, a pair is donated to a child in need. This business model exemplifies purpose-driven innovation by directly addressing social issues while simultaneously creating a profitable enterprise. The company has demonstrated that aligning innovation with social responsibility can lead to both business success and meaningful impact.

Danone: Prioritizing Health and Well-being

Danone has positioned itself as a leader in health-focused products, driven by its mission to bring health through food to as many people as possible. The company's innovation strategy includes developing products that are not only nutritious but also cater to diverse consumer needs across different cultures. Its commitment to purpose-driven innovation has solidified its reputation as a trusted brand in the food industry.

Examining future trends and directions, innovation will increasingly demand a focus on purpose. Consumers are becoming more discerning, prioritizing brands that align with their values. Businesses that fail to recognize this shift may find themselves at a competitive disadvantage. Conversely, organizations that embrace purpose-driven innovation will not only meet consumer expectations but will also contribute positively to society. There are trends to watch out for namely;

Sustainability: As climate change continues to be a pressing issue, businesses will need to innovate in ways that minimize environmental impact. This includes adopting circular economic principles and developing sustainable product lines.

Social Equity:

Purpose-driven innovation will increasingly address social justice issues, ensuring that marginalized communities have access to the same products and services as others.

Technological Integration: Advances in technology will offer new avenues for innovation that align with purpose. For instance, artificial intelligence can be harnessed to develop personalized solutions that cater to individual health needs.

Collaborative Ecosystems: The future of innovation will likely see more partnerships between businesses, non-profits, and governments to tackle complex societal challenges. Collaborative ecosystems can pool resources and expertise to drive impactful change.

Fostering a culture of innovation for the right reasons is not without its challenges. It requires a fundamental shift in mindset, practices, and metrics. However, the rewards are substantial. By aligning innovation with purpose, organizations can create products and services that not only meet market needs but also contribute to a better world. As entrepreneurs, we have the opportunity and the responsibility to lead this charge through our solutions. By championing purpose-driven innovation, we can build businesses that not only generate profits but also leave a lasting, positive impact on society. This is a core value in building purpose-driven profits in our frameworks.

CHAPTER NINE

Ethical Leadership and Decision Making

Leadership is not reserved for a certain class of individuals or c-suite executives. As long as you head a structure no matter how small or are a team lead in a unit or an employee working on a project, you are a leader. In a world increasingly characterized by complexity and rapid change, the role of ethical leadership has never been more critical. Ethical leaders are not just figureheads; they are the moral compass of their organizations, guiding teams through challenging decisions while remaining committed to a purpose-driven mission. This chapter explores the significance of ethical leadership in nurturing a culture of integrity, transparency, and accountability within purpose-driven organizations.

The Foundations of Ethical Leadership

Ethical leadership involves leading by example, where a leader's actions, decisions, and communication reflect a commitment to ethical principles. It encompasses values such as honesty, fairness, respect, and responsibility. Ethical leaders are not only concerned with the bottom line but also with how their decisions affect stakeholders, including employees, customers, and the community.

Values form the bedrock of ethical leadership. They serve as guiding principles that inform decision-making and shape organizational culture. Leaders must articulate and embody these values consistently to instill a sense of trust and integrity among their teams. A clear set of values can also provide a framework for navigating ethical dilemmas, ensuring that decisions align with the organization's purpose.

Some of these values are integrity, accountability, respect, fairness and courage. Integrity is foundational, as ethical leaders uphold honesty and transparency in their actions, fostering trust within the organization. Accountability is equally important; these leaders take responsibility for their decisions and encourage others to do the same, creating a culture of ownership. Respect for the dignity and perspectives of all individuals promote inclusivity and fairness, while fairness ensures equity in decision-making processes, providing equal opportunities and addressing biases. Courage is vital, as ethical leaders stand firm in their beliefs, making difficult choices aligned with moral principles even under pressure.

Compassion reflects their empathy and concern for the well-being of others, extending to both employees and the broader community. They also embrace a service mentality, prioritizing the needs of others and focusing on creating value for stakeholders. Transparency is essential, as ethical leaders openly share information about decisions and processes, fostering collaboration and trust. They encourage innovation, promoting creative problem-solving that aligns with ethical standards and the organization's mission. Finally, a commitment to sustainability drives ethical leaders to adopt practices that promote environmental stewardship and social responsibility, ensuring the long-term health of both the organization and the planet. Together, these values create a robust framework for ethical leadership, guiding leaders in their quest to foster integrity and responsibility within their organizations.

Trust is a cornerstone of this approach to leadership. When leaders demonstrate integrity and transparency, they foster an environment where employees feel safe to express their ideas and concerns. This trust enables open communication and collaboration, allowing for a more agile and responsive organization. Trust also enhances employee engagement and loyalty, as team members are more likely to commit to a leader who prioritizes ethical considerations.

Leaders adopting an ethical approach to managing their teams have tremendous benefits. Such organizations stand the test of time and create the right atmosphere for creating relevant and adoptable solutions. In purpose-driven organizations, ethical leadership is essential for translating purpose into actionable strategies. Leaders must ensure that their organization's mission is not just a statement on a wall but a lived reality. By embodying the organization's purpose in their decisions, ethical leaders inspire employees to align their work with a greater cause, enhancing motivation and engagement.

Individuals heading teams often use a decision-making framework that considers the broader impact of their choices. This framework often includes stakeholder analysis, long-term impact, and ethical principles amongst others.

Stakeholder analysis is a critical step in ethical decision-making, involving a systematic approach to identify and evaluate the interests and influence of various stakeholders. Leaders begin by mapping out all potential stakeholders, which includes internal parties such as employees and management, as well as external groups like customers, suppliers, and community members. Understanding the specific interests, needs, and concerns of each stakeholder is essential, as it helps leaders appreciate diverse perspectives and potential conflicts. Evaluating the influence each stakeholder has over the decision-making process allows leaders to devise effective engagement strategies, such as direct consultations or surveys, to gather valuable feedback. Equally important is the consideration of long-term impact; ethical leaders must adopt a future-oriented mindset that looks beyond immediate results. This involves utilizing scenario analysis to explore various potential outcomes based on different decisions, thereby assessing both risks and opportunities. Incorporating sustainability into this evaluation ensures that decisions align with ethical principles and contribute positively to society. To support this, leaders should establish mechanisms for monitoring long-term effects, setting specific performance metrics related to social and environmental impact.

Integrating these principles into decision-making is vital for maintaining integrity and values. This begins with clearly defining the core ethical principles that guide the organization, such as fairness, transparency, and accountability. When faced with decisions, leaders should evaluate each option against these principles, ensuring alignment with the organization's values. Utilizing established ethical frameworks, such as utilitarianism or virtue ethics, can provide structured ways to analyze ethical implications. Moreover, fostering an environment where ethical dialogue is encouraged allows team members to share their thoughts on potential ethical concerns, reinforcing the importance of ethics in the organizational culture.

Scenario planning involves envisioning various potential futures based on different decisions and their implications. Ethical leaders can use this technique to explore how their choices might play out under various circumstances, considering both best-case and worst-case scenarios. This proactive approach allows leaders to assess the ethical ramifications of their decisions and prepare for potential challenges, ensuring that they remain aligned with the organization's values and purpose.

Consulting and incorporating diverse perspectives into the decision-making process enriches these considerations. Ethical leaders should seek input from a wide range of stakeholders, including employees, customers, community representatives, and experts in relevant fields. This collaborative approach not only fosters inclusivity but also helps leaders understand the broader implications of their decisions, ensuring that different viewpoints and potential impacts are taken into account.

Creating clear ethical guidelines or a decision-making framework can help leaders navigate complex situations. These guidelines should outline key principles and values that the organization stands for, serving as a reference point during decision-making. By having a structured approach that includes criteria for evaluating options against ethical standards, leaders can ensure consistency and alignment with the organization's purpose, making it easier to address dilemmas as they arise.

This structured approach ensures that decisions reflect the organization's values and purpose, reinforcing the commitment to ethical leadership.

Ethical Decision-Making in Practice

Leaders frequently face ethical dilemmas that challenge their values and principles. These dilemmas can arise from competing interests, external pressures, or the pursuit of profitability. Responsible leaders must navigate these challenges with a clear focus on their organization's purpose. For example, consider a company faced with the decision to cut costs by outsourcing production to a country with lower labor standards. While this may improve profit margins in the short term, ethical leaders would weigh the implications for workers, local communities, and the company's reputation. By prioritizing ethical considerations, they can choose a path that aligns with the organization's purpose and values.

Transparent communication is vital in ethical decision-making. Leaders should communicate their rationale for decisions openly and honestly, providing stakeholders with insight into the thought process behind their choices. This transparency helps build trust and fosters a culture of accountability. Moreover, encouraging feedback and dialogue among team members can lead to better decision-making. Ethical leaders should create an environment where employees feel empowered to voice their concerns and suggest alternatives. This inclusive approach not only enhances this method of decision-making but also drives innovation and collaboration.

Cultivating this leadership within organizations is essential for fostering a culture of integrity and trust. As businesses face increasing complexity and stakeholder expectations, the need for leaders who prioritize ethical principles becomes paramount. By embedding these values into the organization's core, leaders can inspire their teams to act responsibly and make informed decisions. Let us examine effective strategies for nurturing and creating this approach to leadership:

Training and Development: To promote ethical leadership, organizations should invest in training and development programs focused on ethics and values. These programs can equip leaders and employees with the tools to recognize ethical dilemmas and make informed decisions that align with the organization's purpose. Topics may include ethical reasoning, conflict resolution, and effective communication.

Mentorship Programs: Establishing mentorship programs can also facilitate the development of ethical leadership. Experienced leaders can guide emerging leaders in navigating ethical challenges and instilling a commitment to values-based decision-making. Mentorship creates a culture of continuous learning and reinforces the importance of ethical behavior across all levels of the organization.

Performance Metrics: Incorporating these considerations into performance metrics is essential for promoting ethical leadership. Organizations should evaluate leaders not only on financial performance but also on their ability to uphold the organization's values and foster a culture of integrity. Metrics could include employee satisfaction scores, stakeholder feedback, and assessments of ethical decision-making.

Case Studies in Ethical Leadership

To further illustrate the impact of ethical leadership, let's examine a few organizations that exemplify this approach.

Johnson & Johnson: A Commitment to Credo

Johnson & Johnson is renowned for its ethical approach to business, rooted in its Credo, a guiding document that outlines the company's responsibilities to various stakeholders. During the 1982 Tylenol crisis, when cyanide-laced capsules led to consumer deaths, the company's leadership demonstrated ethical decision-making by prioritizing customer safety over profits. They swiftly recalled the product and implemented tamper-proof packaging, rebuilding trust and reinforcing their commitment to ethical principles.

Dangote Group

The Dangote Group, led by Aliko Dangote, is one of Africa's largest conglomerates, with operations in various sectors, including cement, sugar, and flour. The company emphasizes corporate social responsibility (CSR) and ethical business practices. This Group invests significantly in community development projects, such as education and healthcare initiatives, demonstrating its commitment to improving the quality of life in the communities where it operates. The company's leadership actively engages with stakeholders to address social and environmental challenges, reinforcing its purpose-driven approach.

Access Bank

Access Bank is a leading financial institution in Nigeria that has established itself as a champion of ethical banking practices. The bank prioritizes sustainability and social impact in its operations, offering products that promote financial inclusion. Access Bank's leadership is committed to environmental, social, and governance (ESG) criteria, and the bank has launched various initiatives to support community development, including educational programs and environmental conservation efforts. This commitment has positioned this bank as a responsible leader in the banking sector.

Safaricom

Safaricom, Kenya's largest telecommunications company, is known for its innovative mobile money service, M-Pesa, which has transformed access to financial services for millions of Kenyans. The company's leadership emphasizes ethical practices and community engagement. The organization has implemented various CSR initiatives, focusing on education, health, and environmental sustainability. The company actively seeks to create social value alongside financial success, aligning its business objectives with the needs of the community.

Bidco Africa

This business is a leading manufacturer of consumer goods, including food and personal care products. The company is recognized for its commitment to ethical business practices and sustainability. Its leadership has implemented initiatives to reduce its environmental footprint and promote sustainable sourcing of raw materials. The company engages with local communities through various programs aimed at improving health, education, and livelihoods. By prioritizing ethical standards and corporate social responsibility, Bidco Africa demonstrates how businesses can succeed while positively impacting society.

Starbucks

This company is well known for its legendary coffee has consistently demonstrated ethical leadership through its commitment to social responsibility. The company has implemented fair trade practices, sustainable sourcing, and community engagement initiatives. By integrating these values into its business model, Starbucks has not only driven profits but also built a loyal customer base that appreciates its commitment to ethical practices.

Patagonia

Patagonia exemplifies purpose-driven leadership by embedding environmental stewardship into its business strategy. The company openly communicates its commitment to sustainability and encourages customers to engage in eco-friendly practices. Patagonia's leadership decisions reflect a strong ethical stance, ensuring that its innovations align with its mission to protect the planet.

Challenges to Ethical Leadership

Despite the importance of ethical leadership, several challenges can hinder its effectiveness within organizations. Leaders often face external pressures, conflicting stakeholder interests, and the complexities of diverse cultural norms that complicate ethical decision-making. Additionally, the rapid pace of change in today's business environment can create ethical blind spots and reputational risks. Understanding these challenges is crucial for developing strategies to overcome them and strengthen the commitment to ethical leadership.

Navigating External Pressures: Responsible leaders often face external pressures that can challenge their commitment to ethical decision-making. These pressures may arise from market competition, investor expectations, or shifting consumer demands. In such situations, ethical leaders must remain steadfast in their principles, prioritizing the long-term interests of the organization and its stakeholders over short-term gains.

Addressing Ethical Blind Spots: Organizations can also fall victim to ethical blind spots such as situations where leaders and employees may overlook ethical implications due to cognitive biases or groupthink. To combat this, ethical leaders should encourage diverse perspectives and foster an environment where ethical concerns can be openly discussed. Regular ethical audits and scenario planning can help identify potential blind spots and ensure that ethical considerations remain at the forefront of decision-making.

Maintaining Accountability: This leadership requires a commitment to accountability. Leaders must hold themselves and their teams accountable for their decisions and actions. This involves acknowledging mistakes, learning from them, and making amends when necessary. A culture of accountability reinforces ethical behavior and demonstrates to employees that ethical leadership is a shared responsibility.

Balancing Stakeholder Interests: Ethical leaders often face the difficult task of balancing the competing interests of various stakeholders, including shareholders, employees, customers, and the community. Each group may have different priorities and expectations, making it challenging for leaders to find solutions that satisfy everyone. Ethical leaders must navigate these complexities while remaining true to the organization's core values and purpose, which can lead to tough decisions and potential conflicts.

Navigating Cultural Differences: In an increasingly globalized business environment, ethical leaders must contend with diverse cultural norms and values. What is considered ethical behavior in one culture may not hold the same significance in another. This cultural diversity can create confusion and challenges when establishing a unified ethical framework across international teams. Ethical leaders must cultivate cultural sensitivity and awareness, ensuring that their decisions are respectful and appropriate in various contexts.

Managing Reputation Risks: In the digital age, information travels quickly, and public perception can change rapidly. Ethical leaders must be vigilant in managing their organization's reputation, as even small missteps can lead to significant backlash. This heightened scrutiny can create pressure to prioritize public image over ethical considerations, especially in crisis situations. Leaders must remain steadfast in their commitment to ethical practices, ensuring that their responses align with their values and maintain stakeholder trust.

What is the future of ethical leadership in business operations and even other sectors? As we move into a future characterized by increased scrutiny and awareness of corporate practices, the demand for ethical leadership will only grow. Organizations that prioritize ethical leadership will be better equipped to navigate challenges, build trust, and create lasting value for all stakeholders.

The standards and expectations surrounding ethical leadership are continually evolving as well. As society grapples with issues such as climate change, social justice, and economic inequality, ethical leaders will need to adapt and respond proactively. This may involve engaging with stakeholders to understand their concerns, incorporating sustainability into business strategies, and advocating for policies that promote equity and justice. Technology can also play a role in enhancing ethical leadership. Tools that promote transparency, such as blockchain for supply chain accountability or data analytics for ethical decision-making, can empower leaders to make informed choices. Additionally, digital platforms can facilitate open communication and feedback, enabling organizations to foster a culture of ethical awareness and engagement.

Ethical leadership is not a destination but a continuous process that requires commitment, reflection, and adaptability. As leaders, we must recognize the profound impact of our decisions on our organizations and society. By embodying ethical principles, we can guide our teams toward a purpose-driven future, ensuring that our organizations thrive while making a positive contribution to the world.

As the complexities of the business settings unfold and each individual strives to adapt, let us remain steadfast in our commitment to ethical leadership. It is through our actions, decisions, and values that we will shape the future of purpose-driven organizations, creating a legacy of integrity and impact for generations to come. The journey may be challenging, but the rewards such as trust, loyalty, and lasting success are well worth the effort.

CHAPTER TEN

Marketing With Purpose

Marketing is all about getting the right message about a product or service to the right people at the right time. It is how we (brands and companies) let customers know what we are selling and why they might want it. Think of it like promoting a band where you create buzz, share what makes the music unique, and connect with fans in a way that gets them excited to listen or buy tickets. It involves understanding what people want and making them aware of what you have to offer. In this era where consumers are increasingly seeking brands that resonate with their values, marketing with purpose has emerged as a crucial strategy for businesses. This chapter delves into the principles of authentic marketing that not only highlight an organization's mission but also engage audiences on a deeper level. By integrating purpose into marketing strategies, businesses can foster genuine connections with customers, enhance brand loyalty, and ultimately drive purpose-driven profits.

What is Marketing with Purpose

Purpose-driven marketing is a strategy that aligns a brand's messaging and activities with its core mission and values. Unlike traditional marketing that primarily focuses on selling products or services, purpose-driven marketing emphasizes the positive impact a brand seeks to make in society. This approach resonates with consumers who are increasingly motivated by ethical considerations and social responsibility, leading to a more engaged and loyal customer base.

Today's consumers are more informed and discerning than ever before. They seek transparency, authenticity, and a sense of connection with the brands they choose. This shift in expectations has transformed the marketing landscape; consumers are less likely to support brands that merely tout their products without demonstrating a commitment to meaningful causes. As a result, organizations must embrace purpose-driven marketing as a means to build trust and foster relationships that go beyond transactional interactions.

There are several strategies organizations can employ to achieve authentic marketing, such as:

Clearly Articulate Your Mission: To effectively market with purpose, organizations must begin by clearly articulating their mission and values. This involves crafting a compelling narrative that encapsulates what the organization stands for and the impact it seeks to achieve.

Mission Statement: Develop a concise mission statement that reflects the organization's core values and purpose. This statement should serve as the foundation for all marketing efforts, guiding messaging and initiatives.

Storytelling: Use storytelling techniques to bring your mission to life. Share real stories of how your organization is making a difference, whether through customer testimonials, case studies, or impact reports. Stories evoke emotions and help audiences connect with your brand on a personal level.

Content is a powerful tool for purpose-driven marketing. By creating meaningful and relevant content, organizations can engage their audience and convey their mission effectively. For instance, a brand can test educational content or user generated content. They can also decide to integrate both styles.

In educational content, you develop content that educates your audience about the issues related to your mission. This could include blog posts, videos, podcasts, or info graphics that raise awareness and provide valuable insights. User-Generated content on the other hand encourages your audience to share their experiences and engage with your brand. User-generated content not only builds community but also reinforces your mission through authentic voices.

Social media platforms provide a dynamic space for purpose-driven marketing, allowing organizations to connect with their audience in real time. You can leverage the immense possibilities of these platforms through engagement, campaigns and building a personal brand. Actively engage with your audience by responding to comments, sharing user-generated content, and participating in conversations related to your mission. This interaction fosters a sense of community and loyalty. Launch social media campaigns that align with your mission. For example, a brand focused on sustainability could run a campaign encouraging customers to share their eco-friendly practices. Such initiatives not only promote engagement but also amplify your purpose.

The need to collaborate with like-minded organizations cannot be overstated. Partnering with organizations that share similar values can enhance your marketing efforts and broaden your reach. These can be achieved through exploring co-branding opportunities with like-minded companies or nonprofits. Joint initiatives can create a powerful impact and showcase your commitment to your mission. Organizations can also collaborate on community service projects or events that resonate with your audience. This hands-on approach allows you to demonstrate your mission in action, further solidifying your brand's purpose.

To build credibility and trust, organizations must measure the impact of their purpose-driven initiatives and share the results with their audience. As earlier mentioned, ensure your typical KPIs have components such as impact metrics embedded into them. Define key performance indicators (KPIs) related to your mission, such as community engagement, environmental impact, or social change. Regularly assess and report on these metrics to showcase your organization's progress. Be transparent about both successes and challenges. Sharing lessons learned reinforces authenticity and builds trust with your audience.

The need to engage your audience is imperative as it can grow potential customers and maintain the right brand reputation. The first step in effectively engaging your audience is because organizations must first understand who they are and what motivates them. This can be discovered through:

Audience Research: Conduct thorough research to identify the values, preferences, and behaviors of your target audience. Use surveys, focus groups, and social media analytics to gain insights into what resonates with them.

Segmentation: Segment your audience based on shared values or interests. Tailoring your marketing efforts to different segments allows for more personalized and relevant messaging.

Purpose-driven marketing thrives on emotional connections. By appealing to the values and beliefs of your audience, organizations can foster loyalty and advocacy. This can be done through:

Values Alignment: Highlight the ways in which your brand's mission aligns with the values of your audience. This alignment creates a sense of belonging and encourages consumers to support your brand.

Authentic Communication: Use authentic and relatable language in your marketing communications. Avoid jargon or overly polished messaging; instead, aim for a tone that reflects genuine passion for your mission.

Engaging your audience goes beyond awareness; it involves encouraging active participation and advocacy. This can include clear calls to action in your marketing efforts that invite your audience to get involved. This could be participating in a campaign, attending an event, or supporting a cause related to your mission. It could also involve implementing loyalty programs that reward customers for supporting your mission. This could include discounts for eco-friendly practices or donations to charitable organizations in their name.

Overcoming Challenges in Purpose-Driven Marketing

Challenges are bound to come up while implementing this concept. Let us explore some issues and how to overcome them.

Navigating Skepticism: One of the primary challenges of purpose-driven marketing is overcoming consumer skepticism. With many brands attempting to align themselves with social causes, consumers may be wary of perceived "green washing" or insincerity. To solve this, ensure that your marketing efforts are rooted in genuine commitment. Avoid superficial campaigns that lack substance; instead, focus on initiatives that reflect your organization's true values. Foster open dialogue with your audience.

Encourage feedback and be responsive to concerns about your marketing efforts. This transparency can help alleviate skepticism and build trust.

Measuring Impact: Another challenge is effectively measuring the impact of purpose-driven initiatives. Organizations may struggle to quantify their contributions to social or environmental causes. Establish clear metrics that align with your mission. These could include qualitative measures, such as community feedback, alongside quantitative data, like the number of lives impacted or resources saved. Share impact reports with your audience, detailing the outcomes of your initiatives. This transparency not only reinforces credibility but also demonstrates your organization's commitment to continuous improvement.

Balancing Profitability and Purpose: Striking the balance between profitability and purpose can be challenging. Organizations may worry that focusing too heavily on purpose-driven initiatives could detract from financial performance. Integrate purpose into your overall business strategy rather than viewing it as a separate initiative. This alignment ensures that purpose and profitability work hand in hand, enhancing brand value and customer loyalty. Adopt a long-term perspective on success. While purpose-driven initiatives may not yield immediate financial returns, they can lead to greater brand loyalty, customer retention, and ultimately, sustainable profits over time.

Case Studies in Purpose-Driven Marketing

Let us see briefly how various companies are incorporating this approach in their marketing tactics.

Patagonia (USA): Known for its commitment to environmental sustainability, Patagonia actively promotes its mission to protect the planet. They engage in campaigns like "Don't Buy This Jacket," encouraging consumers to think about their consumption habits.

TOMS (Global): TOMS is famous for its "One for One" model, where for every pair of shoes sold, they donate a pair to someone in need. This approach emphasizes social impact and resonates with customers who value giving back.

Unilever (Europe): With brands like Dove, Unilever focuses on social issues, such as body positivity and sustainability. Their campaigns, like the Dove Real Beauty campaign, challenge societal norms and promote self-acceptance.

Warby Parker (USA): This eyewear company has a "Buy a Pair, give a Pair" program, donating glasses to those in need for every pair sold. Their mission blends social impact with stylish products, appealing to socially conscious consumers.

Coca-Cola (Global): Coca-Cola's "World Without Waste" initiative aims to collect and recycle a bottle for everyone sold by 2030. Their marketing emphasizes sustainability and community engagement, aligning their brand with environmental goals.

Nedbank (South Africa): Nedbank focuses on sustainability with campaigns like "Greenbacks," promoting environmentally friendly banking practices. They aim to make a positive impact through initiatives that support renewable energy and conservation.

Ecoligo (Ghana): Ecoligo is a solar energy company that connects investors with businesses in emerging markets to fund solar projects. Their marketing highlights the importance of renewable energy in driving economic development and improving lives in underserved communities.

M-Pesa (Kenya): This mobile money platform has transformed financial inclusion in Kenya. The company's marketing emphasizes empowerment, allowing users to access banking services, send money, and make payments, which has significantly improved livelihoods.

Soko (Kenya): Soko connects artisans in Kenya with global consumers, emphasizing fair trade and ethical sourcing. Their marketing focuses on empowering local communities and promoting handcrafted products that reflect cultural heritage.

Lafarge Africa: This building materials company has initiatives focused on sustainable construction and community development. Their marketing highlights environmentally friendly products and efforts to reduce carbon emissions, positioning them as a leader in sustainable building practices.

These companies illustrate how purpose-driven marketing can resonate with consumers and contribute to social and environmental betterment across the African continent.

As consumers increasingly seek brands that align with their values, purpose-driven marketing is poised to play a pivotal role in shaping the future of business. Organizations that successfully integrate purpose into their marketing strategies can build deeper connections with their audiences, enhance brand loyalty, and drive sustainable profits. By clearly articulating their mission, creating meaningful content, and engaging authentically with their customers, businesses can cultivate a marketing approach that resonates on both emotional and ethical levels. It is evident that the commitment to marketing with purpose will not only define brand success but also contribute to a more responsible and sustainable marketplace.

CHAPTER ELEVEN

Scaling Sustainably

In the quest for growth, many companies face a critical challenge: how to expand their operations while remaining true to their core mission and values. Scaling sustainably is not just about increasing profits; it's about creating a lasting impact that aligns with your purpose. This chapter explores approaches to growth that honors your foundational beliefs, ensuring that your expansion enhances your brand's integrity and deepens your societal impact.

How do I Scale Sustainably

At the heart of any purpose-driven organization are its core values. These values should serve as guiding principles for every aspect of your business, especially as you scale. As you plan for expansion, revisit your mission statement and core values. Ensure that every growth strategy aligns with these principles. This alignment fosters a cohesive brand image and builds trust among stakeholders. For instance, if sustainability is a core value, consider how new products or services can enhance rather than dilute this commitment.

Involve your employees, customers, and community members in discussions about your values. Regularly soliciting their input ensures that your values resonate with those who matter most. This can be achieved through surveys, workshops, and community forums, allowing for a shared sense of ownership over the company's mission.

Collaborations can amplify your impact and resources, allowing for a more extensive reach without compromising your purpose. Seek out partnerships with like-minded organizations that share your values. This could include nonprofits, other businesses, or community organizations. For example, a company focused on reducing plastic waste might partner with a local recycling initiative to promote awareness and collective action. Consider collaborating with social enterprises that are already making strides in areas you want to impact. By co-creating programs, you can leverage their expertise and networks while reinforcing your commitment to social good.

Prioritizing the needs of the communities in which you operate can foster loyalty and drive sustainable growth. This can be achieved through:

Local Focus: As you expand, emphasize local hiring and sourcing. This not only supports the local economy but also builds stronger community ties. For instance, a food brand might source ingredients from local farmers, promoting both freshness and community support.

Feedback Mechanisms: Implement systems for gathering community feedback. This could involve regular surveys or community advisory boards. Understanding the needs and desires of your community will allow you to adapt your offerings to better serve them.

Supporting Local Initiatives: Invest in local community projects or initiatives that align with your brand values. This could include sponsoring local events, supporting education programs, or participating in community development projects. Such involvement demonstrates your commitment to the community and helps build goodwill.

Creating Economic Opportunities: Develop programs that provide training and resources for local entrepreneurs or small businesses. By fostering entrepreneurship in the community, you not only empower individuals but also contribute to the overall economic health of the area, creating a mutually beneficial relationship.

Crisis Response and Support: Be proactive in responding to community needs during crises, such as natural disasters or economic downturns. This could involve providing financial support, donating products, or offering services that help the community recover. Such actions reinforce your commitment and build strong, lasting relationships with community members.

Creating products with sustainability in mind is crucial for purpose-driven scaling. Consider the entire lifecycle of your products which runs from sourcing to disposal. Strive for sustainable materials and processes that minimize environmental impact. This could involve using biodegradable packaging or sourcing raw materials from responsible suppliers. Educate your customers about the benefits of your sustainable products. Sharing stories about the positive impacts of their choices can enhance customer loyalty and encourage more responsible consumption.

In today's digital age, technology can be a powerful ally in sustainable scaling. Utilize data analytics to understand customer needs and track the effectiveness of your sustainability initiatives. This insight can guide your growth strategies, ensuring they align with both market demands and your mission.

Use digital marketing and e-commerce to reach broader audiences without the environmental costs associated with traditional retail. This approach allows for scalability while maintaining a commitment to sustainability. Implement automation tools in your operations to improve efficiency and reduce waste. Technologies like smart inventory management systems can optimize resource use and minimize excess, leading to a lower environmental impact while enhancing profitability. Explore the use of block chain technology to increase transparency in your supply chain. By providing a secure and immutable record of transactions, block chain can help trace the origin of materials and ensure ethical sourcing. This level of transparency can strengthen consumer trust and showcase your commitment to sustainability.

Establishing clear metrics for success ensures that your growth remains aligned with your purpose. Develop KPIs that reflect both financial performance and social or environmental impact. Regularly assess these metrics to ensure that your growth strategies are on track and adjust them as needed. Share impact reports with stakeholders to build trust and accountability. By communicating both successes and challenges, you reinforce your commitment to transparency and continuous improvement.

Your internal culture is crucial for sustainable scaling. The teams hold and support your framework as they engage with your customers regularly and run your operations. To build sustainably, you need to ensure that they are carried along and understand the meaning behind adopting this approach.

Foster a culture where employees feel connected to the mission. Encourage them to contribute ideas for sustainable practices and growth strategies. Recognizing their contributions can enhance motivation and loyalty. Implement training that emphasizes the importance of purpose-driven growth. Equip employees with the skills they need to advocate for sustainability within their roles, ensuring that your values permeate every level of the organization.

Navigating Challenges

As with any growth strategy, challenges will arise. There may be times when profitability and mission-driven goals conflict. Develop strategies to navigate these tensions. For instance, consider whether a temporary sacrifice in profit might lead to greater long-term benefits for your brand and mission. Stay agile and be prepared to adjust your growth strategies in response to market trends and consumer preferences. Flexibility will allow you to remain relevant and purposeful in a changing environment.

Finally, having a long-term vision is crucial for sustainable growth. Envision where you want your company to be in the next 5 to 10 years. Ensure that your growth strategies are not just about immediate gains but also about building a sustainable future. Focus on creating a lasting legacy that reflects your purpose. This mindset will guide decision-making and inspire others in the industry to adopt similar practices.

One of the most effective ways to scale sustainably is to view your customers not just as buyers but as partners in your mission. Involve customers in your sustainability efforts by encouraging them to participate in programs like recycling initiatives, product returns, or community service events. This creates a sense of shared responsibility and reinforces their connection to your brand. For example, a company might host clean-up days or tree-planting events where customers can volunteer, thereby deepening their commitment to the brand's purpose.

Establish channels for customer feedback, allowing them to share their experiences and suggestions regarding your products and sustainability efforts. This two-way communication not only helps improve your offerings but also fosters loyalty as customers feel valued and heard. Utilize social media, surveys, and focus groups to actively seek input, ensuring customers see their feedback reflected in product development and company practices.

In an increasingly interconnected world, being aware of and responsive to global trends can enhance your sustainable scaling efforts. Regularly conduct market research to identify global sustainability trends, consumer preferences, and emerging technologies. This insight can inform your product development and marketing strategies, ensuring that they are aligned with what is relevant in the broader context. For example, staying updated on innovations in sustainable materials can help you integrate them into your product line.

As you expand into new markets, be mindful of cultural differences and local sustainability challenges. Tailor your approach to meet the unique needs of each region, demonstrating respect for local customs and practices while promoting your purpose. Understanding local attitudes toward sustainability can help you craft marketing messages that resonate more deeply and foster stronger connections with new audiences.

Building a Resilient Supply Chain

A sustainable and resilient supply chain is essential for scaling your business while maintaining your purpose. Prioritize sourcing materials and products from suppliers that share your commitment to sustainability. This can involve evaluating suppliers based on their environmental practices, labor conditions, and ethical standards. Building relationships with responsible suppliers not only supports your mission but can also enhance your brand reputation.

Foster transparency within your supply chain by openly communicating your sourcing practices and the environmental and social impacts of your products. This could involve sharing stories about your suppliers and their contributions to sustainability. By being transparent, you build trust with customers and stakeholders, allowing them to understand and appreciate your commitment to ethical practices. To increase resilience, diversify your supplier base to mitigate risks associated with dependency on a single source. This can protect your operations from disruptions caused by natural disasters, economic shifts, or political instability. A diverse supply chain can also enhance your ability to respond to changing consumer demands for sustainability.

Whenever possible, consider local sourcing to reduce transportation emissions and support local economies. Building relationships with local suppliers not only decreases your carbon footprint but also strengthens community ties. Highlighting these local partnerships in your marketing can resonate with consumers who prioritize community impact.

Innovation is necessary to sustaining growth and adapting to changing market conditions while staying true to your purpose. Create an internal culture that encourages employees to develop innovative solutions for sustainability challenges. This can be achieved through hackathons, brainstorming sessions, or dedicated sustainability teams. Recognizing and rewarding innovative ideas can motivate staff to think outside the box and contribute to your mission.

Allocate resources to research and development focused on sustainable practices and products. This investment can lead to breakthroughs that enhance your offerings while minimizing environmental impact. By staying at the forefront of sustainability innovation, you position your brand as a leader in your industry and attract customers who prioritize eco-friendly choices. Seek out partnerships with startups and innovators in the sustainability space. Collaborating with these organizations can bring fresh ideas and technologies to your business, helping you stay ahead of trends and improve your sustainability initiatives. This can also enhance your brand's image as a forward-thinking leader in the market.

Engage your customers in the innovation process by soliciting their input on product development and sustainability initiatives. Creating platforms for customer feedback, such as surveys or co-creation workshops, allows you to tap into their insights and preferences. This collaborative approach can lead to products that better meet consumer needs while aligning with your sustainability goals.

Scaling sustainably is a multifaceted journey that requires careful consideration of your core values, community impact, and long-term vision. By embracing innovative partnerships, leveraging technology, and cultivating a purpose-driven culture, you can achieve growth that not only benefits your business but also contributes positively to society and the environment. Remember, sustainable success is not merely about financial metrics; it's about making a meaningful impact that endures beyond the bottom line.

CHAPTER TWELEVE

The Future of Purpose-Driven Business

In recent years, the concept of purpose-driven business has transcended from being a niche idea to a fundamental pillar of corporate strategy. As companies increasingly recognize the importance of aligning their operations with a greater societal good, the landscape of entrepreneurship is evolving. This chapter explores the current trends shaping purpose-driven businesses, the technological advancements fueling this movement, and the challenges that lie ahead. By examining these elements, we can gain insights into the future of business in a world where purpose is paramount.

Current Trends in Purpose-Driven Business

The rise of purpose-driven entrepreneurship is evident across various sectors, driven by a collective shift in consumer expectations and societal values.

Social entrepreneurship represents a fundamental shift in the traditional business model, where the primary goal is no longer solely profit maximization. Companies are increasingly being established to address social, environmental, and cultural challenges. This paradigm shift has led to the emergence of numerous organizations dedicated to creating positive impact alongside financial sustainability. Take TOMS Shoes, for example. The company built its brand on the promise that for every pair of shoes sold, another pair would be donated to a child in need. This model not only creates a direct social impact but also fosters strong customer loyalty and brand advocacy. Similar models are being adopted across various industries, from sustainable fashion brands to social enterprises focused on clean water initiatives.

Millennials and Generation Z are now significant players in the consumer market, and their purchasing power is substantial. These generations prioritize brands that reflect their values and are committed to social and environmental issues. Research shows that over 70% of young consumers are willing to switch brands if they find one that aligns better with their personal beliefs. Brands like Patagonia have thrived by taking bold stances on environmental issues, successfully cultivating a community of loyal customers who appreciate the company's commitment to sustainability. The younger generations are not just consumers; they are advocates for change, and they expect the brands they support to contribute positively to society.

In today's information age, consumers demand transparency from the brands they support. They are more informed than ever about supply chains, labor practices, and environmental impacts and they hold companies accountable for their actions. This demand for transparency has prompted businesses to adopt more ethical practices and ensure that their operations align with their stated values.

The B Corp certification, which recognizes companies meeting high standards of social and environmental performance, accountability, and transparency, has become a hallmark for businesses striving to demonstrate their commitment to purpose. Consumers are increasingly seeking out these certifications, further emphasizing the need for businesses to substantiate their claims with concrete actions.

Leading companies are no longer treating purpose as an ancillary component of their business model; they are embedding it into their core strategies. This integration often leads to innovation and growth, as teams are encouraged to think creatively about how their work can contribute to the greater good. Unilever's Sustainable Living Plan exemplifies this approach. By embedding sustainability into its brand portfolio, Unilever guides product innovation and marketing strategies across its diverse range of offerings. This strategy not only aligns with consumer expectations but also enhances brand equity and resilience in a competitive marketplace.

As the landscape of purpose-driven business evolves, we are witnessing a rise in partnerships between purpose-driven companies and nonprofit organizations, government entities, and even competitors. Collaborative efforts can amplify impact and create change on a larger scale than any single entity could achieve alone. The United Nations Sustainable Development Goals (SDGs) provide a framework for cross-sector collaboration, encouraging businesses to align their strategies with global objectives. By fostering these partnerships, companies can leverage resources, share knowledge, and enhance their overall impact in addressing pressing social and environmental challenges.

Technology is a powerful enabler of purpose-driven initiatives, providing tools and platforms that help businesses achieve their social and environmental goals. Data analytics allows companies to measure their impact and optimize their operations for greater efficiency and effectiveness. By harnessing big data, organizations can assess their contributions to social issues, from tracking carbon footprints to evaluating community engagement efforts.

For instance, companies like Salesforce have integrated social impact metrics into their platforms, allowing users to measure the effectiveness of their initiatives in real-time. This not only enhances transparency but also fosters accountability, enabling businesses to refine their strategies based on data-driven insights.

Social media platforms have become essential tools for purpose-driven businesses, providing a space to advocate for social and environmental issues while engaging directly with consumers. Brands can share their missions, tell impactful stories, and mobilize communities around causes they care about. A prime example is Ben & Jerry's, which actively uses its social media channels to advocate for social justice issues, from climate change to racial equality. By leveraging these platforms, the brand not only builds a loyal customer base but also drives awareness and action around critical social issues.

Regulatory and Economic Factors

As the business landscape shifts, so too do the regulatory and economic factors influencing purpose-driven companies. Governments worldwide are increasingly adopting regulations that promote sustainable practices and corporate responsibility. These regulations often encourage businesses to adopt greener practices, invest in sustainable technologies, and prioritize ethical labor practices. For example, the European Union's Green Deal aims to make Europe the first climate-neutral continent by 2050, incentivizing companies to reduce their carbon emissions and invest in sustainable innovation. As regulatory frameworks evolve, purpose-driven businesses that prioritize sustainability will not only comply with regulations but also position themselves as industry leaders.

Impact investing is gaining momentum, with investors seeking to fund businesses that prioritize social and environmental impact alongside financial returns. The rise of Environmental, Social, and Governance (ESG) criteria has led to increased scrutiny of companies' practices and performance. Investors are increasingly favoring companies that demonstrate a strong commitment to purpose, viewing these businesses as more resilient and likely to succeed in the long term. Firms that prioritize ESG factors are better positioned to attract investment and maintain their competitive edge.

While the future of purpose-driven business is promising, several challenges remain that entrepreneurs and leaders must navigate.

As purpose-driven business becomes more mainstream, the risk of "purpose-washing" which is where companies exaggerate or misrepresent their commitment to social and environmental issues has emerged. This practice can lead to consumer skepticism and damage brand credibility. To mitigate this risk, companies must ensure that their purpose is genuine and supported by meaningful actions. Transparency and accountability are essential to building trust with consumers and stakeholders.

Finding the right balance between profit and purpose can be challenging. Businesses must navigate the tension between achieving financial goals and making a positive impact. Leaders should cultivate a mindset that sees profit and purpose as complementary rather than mutually exclusive. Companies that successfully integrate purpose into their business models often find that their commitment to social and environmental issues enhances their brand reputation and drives customer loyalty, ultimately leading to long-term profitability.

As consumers become more discerning, businesses must navigate skepticism surrounding their purpose-driven initiatives. Stakeholders are increasingly demanding evidence of impact and accountability, which requires companies to invest in measurement and reporting. Building a culture of transparency and engaging stakeholders in meaningful dialogue can help companies address skepticism and demonstrate their commitment to purpose.

Visionary leadership plays a crucial role in the success of purpose-driven businesses. Leaders must cultivate a culture that prioritizes purpose and empowers employees to contribute to the organization's mission. Leaders should strive to create a workplace culture that embraces purpose as a guiding principle. This involves fostering an environment where employees feel connected to the company's mission and are motivated to contribute to positive change.

Companies like Zappos have successfully cultivated a strong organizational culture that emphasizes purpose and values. By empowering employees to engage with the community and contribute to social initiatives, Zappos has built a loyal workforce that is committed to the company's mission. Leaders like Howard Schultz of Starbucks and Rose Marcario of Patagonia have exemplified how purpose-driven leadership can drive success. By prioritizing social impact and sustainability, these leaders have built companies that resonate with consumers and create meaningful change. Their commitment to purpose has not only enhanced brand loyalty but has also positioned their companies as leaders in their respective industries.

The future of purpose-driven business is likely to be characterized by the emergence of new industries and sectors focused on purpose.

Emerging Industries and Sectors: As societal needs evolve; we can expect to see the emergence of new industries centered around sustainability and social impact. Renewable energy, waste management, and sustainable agriculture are just a few sectors poised for growth as consumers and businesses increasingly prioritize environmental considerations. Entrepreneurs have the opportunity to innovate within these sectors, creating solutions that address pressing global challenges while building profitable enterprises.

The Evolving Role of Corporate Social Responsibility (CSR): Corporate social responsibility is evolving from a reactive approach to a proactive strategy integrated into core business practices. Companies are now expected to demonstrate their commitment to social and environmental issues not just through philanthropy but by embedding purpose into their operations. This evolution requires businesses to reevaluate their CSR strategies and align them with their overall missions, ensuring that their efforts create meaningful impact.

Predictions for Changing Consumer Behavior: Consumer behavior will continue to shift as younger generations demand greater accountability from brands. Companies that fail to align with consumer values risk losing market share to competitors that prioritize purpose. As awareness of social and environmental issues grows, businesses that authentically commit to purpose will thrive in this evolving landscape.

To succeed in the future of purpose-driven business, organizations must adopt the best practices that integrate purpose into their models.

Integrating Purpose into Business Models: Purpose should be woven into the fabric of business models, influencing every aspect of operations, from product development to marketing strategies. Companies should assess how their offerings contribute to social and environmental goals and adjust accordingly. Engaging employees in this process can foster a sense of ownership and commitment to the company's mission, enhancing overall impact.

To ensure accountability, businesses must establish metrics for measuring their social and environmental impact. This involves developing key performance indicators (KPIs) that align with the organization's purpose and regularly assessing progress.

By transparently sharing these metrics with stakeholders, companies can build trust and demonstrate their commitment to purpose. Engaging stakeholders including employees, customers, and community members is vital for the success of purpose-driven initiatives. Companies should foster open dialogue and collaboration, inviting feedback and input from diverse perspectives. This engagement not only enhances the effectiveness of initiatives but also strengthens relationships and builds a loyal community around the brand.

Globalization and Purpose-Driven Business

As the world becomes more interconnected, purpose-driven businesses are increasingly operating on a global scale. This globalization presents both opportunities and challenges for companies striving to make a positive impact.

Emerging markets offer significant potential for purpose-driven businesses. As economies grow, there is a rising middle class with increasing purchasing power and a desire for sustainable products. Companies that can tailor their offerings to meet the needs of these consumers while addressing local social and environmental issues can gain a competitive edge. For instance, companies like Grameen Bank have successfully operated in developing countries by providing microloans to empower entrepreneurs and lift communities out of poverty. By understanding local contexts and collaborating with local stakeholders, purpose-driven businesses can create meaningful change while expanding their market reach.

Operating globally also requires sensitivity to cultural differences and varying ethical standards. What works in one market may not resonate in another, and companies must be careful to adapt their purpose-driven initiatives accordingly. For example, a brand's commitment to sustainability may be viewed differently across regions. Businesses must engage with local communities to understand their values and expectations, ensuring that their initiatives are culturally relevant and ethically sound. This approach fosters trust and demonstrates genuine commitment to making a positive impact.

Education and awareness are vital in fostering a culture of purpose-driven entrepreneurship. As more individuals become informed about social and environmental issues, the demand for purpose-driven businesses will continue to grow. Educational institutions play a critical role in shaping the next generation of entrepreneurs and business leaders. By incorporating purpose-driven principles into curricula, schools can empower students to think critically about their roles in society and the impact of their future businesses.

Programs that focus on social entrepreneurship, sustainability, and ethical leadership can equip students with the skills and knowledge needed to navigate the complexities of purpose-driven business. Initiatives like the Ashoka U network foster a culture of social innovation in higher education, encouraging students to develop solutions to pressing global challenges.

In parallel, raising awareness among consumers about the importance of supporting purpose-driven businesses is essential. Campaigns that highlight the impact of consumer choices can encourage individuals to seek out brands that align with their values. Social media, community engagement, and storytelling are powerful tools for educating consumers about the benefits of purpose-driven businesses. For example, initiatives like "Buy One, Give One" or "1% for the Planet" create awareness around the tangible impact of supporting socially responsible brands. By fostering a culture of awareness and education, we can create a more informed consumer base that actively seeks out purpose-driven companies, driving further demand for positive change.

The future of purpose-driven business is promising, with the potential to create significant social and environmental impact. As entrepreneurs and business leaders embrace the principles of purpose, they must navigate the challenges and opportunities that lie ahead. By understanding current trends, leveraging technology, and cultivating a strong organizational culture, businesses can thrive while making a meaningful difference in the world. The call to action is clear: embrace the future of purpose-driven entrepreneurship and lead with intention, ensuring that the next generation of businesses prioritizes purpose as a fundamental tenet of success.

ABOUT THE AUTHOR

Damilola Tomiwa Fasinu is an entrepreneur who is passionate about changing lives through her solutions. With a skill for creating purpose-driven ventures, Damilola has successfully scaled her business while prioritizing sustainability and community impact. Her journey is marked by a relentless pursuit of excellence, making her a respected figure in the entrepreneurial sector.

She has a keen ability to identify emerging trends and translate them into actionable strategies, positioning her as a leader in driving meaningful change. Her insights into creating value that resonates with customers are invaluable for individuals seeking to make a lasting impact.

She is not only a successful entrepreneur but also a dedicated mentor and advocate for innovation. She believes in the transformative power of entrepreneurship and actively supports emerging talent through workshops, speaking engagements, and mentorship programs. Her commitment to fostering a collaborative ecosystem encourages others to pursue their passions and build businesses that contribute positively to society.

In Building Purpose-Driven Profits, Damilola shares her wealth of knowledge and experience, offering practical guidance and inspiration for entrepreneurs at any stage of their journey. Her authentic approach blends personal anecdotes with actionable strategies, making this book a vital resource for anyone looking to create a successful, purpose-driven venture. Through her words, she invites readers to explore the intersection of profitability and purpose, empowering them to redefine success on their own terms.

www.ingramcontent.com/pod-product-compliance
Lightning Source LLC
LaVergne TN
LVHW092007090526
838202LV00001B/42